Central America,

Central America, 1821–1871

Liberalism before Liberal Reform

Lowell Gudmundson
Héctor Lindo-Fuentes

The University of Alabama Press
Tuscaloosa and London

designed by zig zeigler

The paper on which this book is printed meets the minimum
requirements of American National Standard for Information
Science-Permanence of Paper for Printed Library Materials,
ANSI Z39.48-1984.

Library of Congress Cataloging-in-Publication Data

Gudmunson, Lowell.
Central America, 1821–1871 : liberalism before liberal reform
/ Lowell Gudmunson, Héctor Lindo-Fuentes.
p.   cm.
Includes bibliographical references and index.
ISBN 0-8173-0765-6
1. Central America—History—1821–1951.   2. Liberalism—
Central America—History—19th century. 3. Central America
—Economic conditions.   I. Lindo-Fuentes, Héctor, 1952–   .
II. Title.
F1438.G95   1995
972.8'04—dc20   94-3593

British Library Cataloguing-in-Publication Data available

iv

Contents

Preface   vii

Introduction   1

    Notes   12

**1. The Economy of Central America:
From Bourbon Reforms to Liberal Reforms
Héctor Lindo-Fuentes**   13

    The Colonial Heritage   14

    From Traditional to Export Agriculture   29

    Export Agriculture and Trade   63

    Conclusion   72

    Notes   76

**2. Society and Politics in Central America, 1821–1871
Lowell Gudmundson**   79

    The Conservative Interlude and Liberal Challenge   81

    From Corn and Cattle to Coffee: Land Tenure Policies   93

    The Church Question: Mortmain and Life's Blood   100

    Secularization and the Clerical Counteroffensive   104

    Society Transformed: Economic and Demographic Bases   110

    Society Redefined: Race Mixture and Ethnic Identity   120

    Conclusion   125

    Notes   128

Suggestions for Further Reading   133

Index   151

Preface

Central America is a small corner of the world, and those who study it form an even smaller clan. Although the authors of this study had each conducted research on nineteenth-century Central America and the impact of coffee (Lindo-Fuentes in El Salvador and Gudmundson in Costa Rica), we had never met at professional conferences in the region or in the United States prior to our involvement in an effort to produce a modern, synthetic history of Central America as part of the Columbian Quincentenary. At two preliminary gatherings of research teams we were genuinely and pleasantly surprised to find that we were both concentrating on the mid-nineteenth century, an exceptionally murky period in local history. We found that we were each struggling toward a comparative framework, that we had each identified some of the same issues as ones of major importance, and that we were in agreement on the need for revisions and the nature of many regionwide processes.

Nevertheless, we did not agree on what those revisions should be in every case. The reader will find separate, individual essays, each written with its own voice, from a different vantage point, and with its own emphases and interpretations. As we presented our hypotheses and arguments to research colleagues at meetings in Costa Rica in 1989 and 1991, we were struck both by their similarities and by the perplexed reactions on the part of colleagues raised on a scholarly diet of essentially Liberal interpretations of the region's history. The curved mirrors of partisan labels have created a great deal of confusion regarding Central American history. Lifting part of the dead weight of a Liberal-inspired orthodoxy from the interpretation of mid-nineteenth-century Central America is the common goal that has brought us together in this interpretive effort.

Earlier versions of the essays that follow were prepared for the six-volume *Historia general de Centroamérica* published by the Latin American Social Science Faculty (FLACSO) in San José, Costa Rica. They appeared in volume 3, edited by Héctor Pérez Brignoli (Madrid: Editorial Siruela/FLACSO, 1993). (The six-volume work was awarded the Costa Rican national history prize for 1993.) We subsequently have

Preface

adapted and revised the texts to suit an English-language audience. We thank FLACSO and its director, Edelberto Torres Rivas, for their support in this endeavor and for their generous permission to publish the work independently in English.

We also thank the staff members of several historical institutions in the region. In Guatemala City, both the Archivo General de Centroamérica and its director, Julio Roberto Gil, and the Biblioteca César Brañas and its director, Carmen Valenzuela de Garay, offered critical assistance. In San Salvador, the staff of the Archivo Nacional, in particular Miguel Angel Sánchez, and the staff members of the Biblioteca de la Universidad Centroamericana (UCA), the Biblioteca Gallardo, and the Biblioteca José Alfaro Durán were extremely helpful during the different stages of research. In Costa Rica the Archivos Nacionales staff and its director, Luz Alba Chacón de Umaña, provided their usual excellent support. Marielos Hernández and Todd Little-Siebold of Tulane University aided in obtaining Guatemalan materials, as did David McCreery, Jim Handy, Chris Lutz, and José Antonio Fernández. Helpful commentary, timely assistance, or both were provided by David Rock, Fernando López Alves, Mario Samper, Héctor Pérez Brignoli, Arturo Taracena, Eric Ching, Fernando Rocchi, and David Flaten. Several of the illustrations were prepared by photographer Thomas Jacob. The map was made by Santiago Echegoyén in El Salvador. To all we give our thanks.

Our home institutions—the University of California, Santa Barbara, Fordham University, the University of Oklahoma, and Mount Holyoke College—have been generous in their support of the research leading to the completion of this study. A Fulbright grant to Gudmundson during 1991 was also instrumental in advancing the work. At The University of Alabama Press we thank Director Malcolm MacDonald for his early interest in the project. We also thank our editor, Kathleen Swain, for her expert help, and we thank the external reviewers for their suggestions for improvements in the work.

Support from family, friends, and colleagues has been no less critical to the completion of this work. Our thanks for their countless contributions is best expressed personally but is also publicly acknowledged here.

Central America, 1821–1871

Introduction

Central America and its ill-fated federation (1824–1839) are often viewed as the archetype of the "anarchy" of early independent Spanish America, and surely a grain of truth can be found in this commonplace view. Nevertheless, in traditional wisdom, this view appears in tandem with another in which the Liberal revolution eventually arrives, after 1871 in Guatemala and Costa Rica and 1879 in El Salvador, to save the day for order and progress, with the intervening period reduced to a dormant "long wait,"[1] when the endless obstacles offered by Conservatives to the Liberal program made progress impossible.

In retrospect, the idea of a "long wait" seems to be a brilliant phrase that blinds the historian rather than illuminates the period. We believe the time is ripe to build a new framework of interpretation for mid-nineteenth-century Central America. We expect to replace this view, an extremely resilient one for reasons that will be explained later, with a more dynamic picture. We will show that, in reality, the Liberal reforms only formalized a situation long in the making. In doing so we downgrade the significance of the reform movement of the 1870s as a turning point in the economic, political, and social history of Central America, however great its historiographic and ideological significance for Liberal historians and statesmen thereafter.

Our efforts are not the product of revisionism for its own sake; instead, the methodical, collective efforts by colleagues in scholarly monographs published over a period of twenty or more years have forced us to consider new problems and to revisit old ones with an open mind. New interpretations for other regions of Latin America also encouraged us to think harder about the fruitful years of the mid-nineteenth century and to bring these elements together in a comprehensive synthesis.

Those who have kept abreast of this growing literature on nineteenth-century Central America may not be surprised with the interpretive thrust presented here. Frankly, however, only a few individuals

1

in the world fall within this category. The reader who is unfamiliar with Central America will find in the following pages both a basic introduction that brings together information scattered in many hard-to-find articles and monographs and a series of critical perspectives on the region and its history.

If the traditional view of the federation struggles is perhaps a well-intentioned half-truth used to exemplify continental difficulties and failures, the idea of sudden changes following the Liberal reforms has a much more purposeful and interesting origin. It was the retrospective judgment of a whole generation of (full-time) Liberal partisans and (part-time) historians from before 1870 to after 1950 throughout the region. The painting of a picture of early independent stasis and squalor inevitably and intentionally cast the Liberal reform era and the societies it generated, increasingly based on export-oriented agriculture (coffee and then bananas), in a particularly favorable light. Indeed, those who developed and inculcated such a view and its underlying periodization in subsequent generations were consciously "building nations" and identifying their idea of nation with a specific economic project that, not surprisingly, favored their class.

The dominant orthodoxy inherited from the late nineteenth-century Liberals held sway throughout the region until at least the early 1960s, when developmental economics and planning for a Central American common market began to challenge, however meekly, free trade, export-led growth strategies. What Liberals saw as progress mid-twentieth-century Marxist and left-wing social scientists saw as economic growth favoring a privileged minority and impoverishing the masses. In making their case, however, they interpolated Liberal orthodoxy, accepting its fundamental parameters in most regards. Central American Marxism proved to be the direct descendant of partisan Liberalism in terms of both its social bases in Hispanic, artisanal, and middle-class groups (also the early foot soldiers of Liberalism) and its revival of classic Liberal issues such as anticlericalism and individual equality before the law.

Historiographically as well, the Marxist Left joined the chorus denouncing the early independent era's supposedly uneventful continuation of (or even regression to) colonial patterns of (neo)-feudal backwardness and exploitation. In their view the Liberal reforms still represented a clear turning point that transformed peasants into a rural proletariat, accelerated the incorporation into world markets, thus increasing dependency, and provided the material basis for an emerging oligarchy of landowners. Contrary to the long-lived orthodoxy in which 1871 acquires a semimystical significance, we would argue for the critical importance of gold rush–era antecedents for both coffee cultivation and the land tenure innovations associated in the popular imagination with Liberal reform. Moreover, we believe that the early independent struggle between Liberals and Conservatives has been profoundly misrepresented both by the victors and by subsequent scholars far too willing to take the partisan epithets and invidious distinctions at something approaching face value. Finally, we believe that the internal economic reorientations associated with Liberal reform, especially export-led growth policies and results, began to emerge as early as the 1840s and were clearly evident by the 1860s nearly everywhere, well before the definitive triumph of partisan Liberalism in the 1870s in Guatemala and El Salvador, the center of gravity of the region both economically and demographically.

The significance of the decades that interest us in this book has begun to emerge from the research of historians such as Ralph Lee Woodward, Jr., David McCreery, and Julio Castellanos Cambranes in Guatemala and Mario Samper Kutschbach and others in Costa Rica (see Suggestions for Further Reading for reference to their major works). They have uncovered evidence with a level of detail that challenges preconceived notions. Their work on the use of land, the impact of export agriculture, the complexity of labor arrangements, and the role of the state has had a cumulative impact, modifying our understanding of the period and encouraging us to engage in this exercise of reinterpretation.

It also seemed time to use our newly acquired knowledge of a richer historical specificity for each country to provide a comparative interpretation that could help us make sense of Central America as a whole. The historiography shows two tendencies in this regard: it either stresses trends common to all of Central America using broad brush strokes that obscure the individuality of each case or concentrates on specific countries without making any substantial effort to refer to what was happening in the others. The comparative framework of our two essays tries to avoid both flattening generalizations and mind-numbing detail.

It is not a coincidence that research on Costa Rica has helped in challenging the basic premises of Liberal orthodoxy and its Marxist sequel. Costa Rica's history is rich in exquisite ironies. It was the first country to export coffee and did so under nominally Conservative leadership. Its rapid incorporation into world markets and the early formation of an export-oriented oligarchy was followed by another feat—it played a key role in the formation of the infamous United Fruit Company, the whipping boy of Marxist and *dependentista* (dependency theorist) alike. Nevertheless, it evolved into a democratic political system with social indices that compare favorably with any other Latin American country, Cuba included. A fortunate by-product of Costa Rica's success was the best higher education system in Central America and the most developed historiography, thus providing an excellent starting point for a serious reinterpretation of Central American history as a whole.

Given the stark contrast between the Costa Rican case and the orthodox Liberal historiography, one wonders why it took so long for the conventional view to be challenged. The common practice has been to deal with Costa Rica only as the "exception" to any regionwide generalization. In addition, part of the problem has been that when historians study periods in which bona fide Conservatives such as Carrera were in power, they tend to pay more attention to the well-known subjects, Church and Indian policies or protectionism, than to "Liberal-regime issues," such as export growth or private forms of land tenure. Nevertheless, all over Central America the material and social class basis for export agriculture emerged under whatever partisan flag. In Costa Rica, then El Salvador, and then Guatemala, it emerged under formally Conservative rule at the time. Elsewhere, in Nicaragua and Honduras, the experience would be part tragedy, part parody, but no amount of fiery rhetoric, dictatorial method, or genuflection before early Liberal icons would translate a Liberal state into an export-driven (Liberal) society. Furthermore, Costa Rica's early entrance in the midcentury boom period of coffee's expansion surely gave it certain advantages in facing the later systemic crises of overproduction and trade disruptions caused by world war and depression. Costa Rica also had the advantage of struggling with key questions of political representation and incorporation within the framework of earlier, classical or romantic Liberalism to some extent before the exclusionary, reactionary, and racist implications of second-generation Liberalism and Positivism emerged full-blown.

Our downsizing of Liberal achievements and consequent challenge to their self-image collides with a highly attractive framework that has appealed to both establishment Liberal and leftist, progressive thought in the isthmus since the revolutions of the 1870s. Our aim, however, goes beyond the simple pleasures of iconoclasm. We hope to provide avenues by which to pursue more adequate solutions to major interpretive problems. We believe that the time is ripe to build a new framework of interpretation for mid-nineteenth-century Central America, based on what we have learned both from the study of primary sources from that period, and from the above-mentioned pioneering studies of the region's history.

If our picture of the pre-1870s Liberals is not a flattering one, neither does it fall into the trap, common to much of the literature, of blaming second-generation, post-1870s Liberals for abandoning or betraying a tradition that we argue did not dominate even in the 1830s, the heyday of romantic Liberalism. The sins of the second generation were legion, perhaps, but betrayal was not the foremost shortcoming.

This view essentially represents an extension and refinement of the pioneering work of Mario Rodríguez on independence-era politics wherein he shows how early nineteenth-century Conservatives were as much children of the Enlightenment as their Liberal opponents.[2] What we propose to show here is that the political contenders not only shared much philosophical and ideological baggage but also sprang from similar class origins. Thus, to view Liberals uniformly as social radicals at midcentury is no more plausible than painting Conservatives as blind reactionaries with a uniquely oligarchic pedigree. Just such a view was militantly asserted by the early Liberals and has been transmitted to successive generations in an unbroken chain of progressive, anti-oligarchic social thought. This overly simplistic and optimistic reading of the Central American past has led to interpretive failures far beyond narrowly historiographic boundaries.

Rethinking the process by which Liberals finally came to rule and rewriting its history, we were struck by the long reach of ideological distortions and the speed of changes in historical imagery as a consequence of successive political and ideological confrontations. Here we find fully borne out E. Bradford Burns's emphasis on the way in which the Liberal preference and prejudice of a whole generation of late nineteenth-century historians in the region profoundly distorted their and our own view of the past.[3]

Our earlier work on cases as politically dissimilar as twentieth-century El Salvador and Costa Rica should have prepared us for the shock. After all, it was precisely the coffee elites of these two countries who, in the second half of the nineteenth century, spoke endlessly of how similar, if not identical, their societies and economies were: Hispanic, enterprising, and trade oriented, with widely distributed property and political participation. Nevertheless, after the mid-twentieth century a virtually identical but now negative correlation between "egalitarian" Costa Rica and "oligarchic" El Salvador became the established wisdom for the earlier period as well.[4]

Contemporary experiences illustrate how perceptions of the past are transformed by events. Witnessing the late twentieth-century transformation of national and ethnic identities, the disintegration of empires and ideologies, and the cosmetic refurbishing and projection of others gives us a healthier respect for the way in which ideological struggle has colored not only subsequent interpretations but also the terms used to discuss any concrete situation. Although our inspiration may come from the context of the late twentieth century, scholars such as Carol Smith, Steven Palmer, and Philippe Bourgois have shown how such insights can be applied to earlier periods as well. Thus, we hope to contribute, however modestly, to the ongoing debate regarding nationality, ethnic identity, and class relationships in nineteenth-century Central America.

Our reinterpretation of this period also can be seen in the context of major revisions under way in Latin American historiography. Our downplaying of the role of dramatic political events and our emphasis on international trade forces and local responses to them, visible from the late 1840s throughout the region, echo the periodization emerging from synthetic works on Latin America as a whole. Bushnell and Macaulay see the midcentury years as a turning point for Latin America when a new policy consensus and changes in international trade, lower freight rates, a new generation of leaders, and greater political stability set the stage for Liberal reforms. Ironically, and as a reflection of the earlier scholarship that they use for their interpretation, Bushnell and Macaulay see Guatemala as "a clear cut exception" to this pattern.[5]

Also in common with recent scholarship on the nineteenth century, we move away from the more rigid and reactive versions of dependency theory and find local elites acting with a great deal of autonomy and understanding of their own interests. Internal processes are explored and given privilege over externally determined ones. Where an earlier

Introduction

literature depicted Conservatives and folk-leader strongmen or caudillos as succumbing to overwhelming external market forces after lengthy, bitter opposition, we believe they themselves shifted policy consistently in the direction of responding to and taking advantage of rather than resisting those forces.

This new scholarship amounts to a virtual shift in paradigm that is still unfolding. The reader should be alerted that, although this change in Latin American historiography may be strengthened by recent political changes, its roots are to be found elsewhere. As Florencia Mallon has stated in a recent essay, the origins of this change in paradigm are to be found, as could be expected from historians, in solid research in primary sources. "By the late 1970s," Mallon writes, "a new trend began to take shape in the historical literature. Some of the researchers trained in the dependency-oriented debates of mid-decade began returning from the field with the kind of empirically rich, regionally specific data that made untenable the new determinism implicit in the *dependentista*-influenced view of the nineteenth century."[6]

Our essays, on the other hand, do not observe Peter Evans and Theda Skocpol's advice to "bring the State back in" as much as they depict politics more broadly than either dramatic events or the sphere of official exercise of power.[7] The issue of the relative autonomy of the state seems elusive in a context of weak states that are only beginning to take shape on the ruins of colonial structures. Advice that may be relevant for Peru or Mexico seems less so for the former subdivisions of the Kingdom of Guatemala. We challenge the view, common to both early nineteenth-century Liberals in Central America and many twentieth-century leftist frameworks, that control of the state through political means alone can ensure the achievement of radical economic ends involving the restructuring of society, that the state as such can achieve goals beyond those of the classes that dispute and control power within it.

On another level, however, our sense of the centrality of "politics," that is, the competition between groups with different interests and views on social structure and economic change (which involves more than the state alone), is actually strengthened. The distribution of power, whatever its source, and the expectations groups had in terms of status, deference, rights, obligations, and opportunities are the keys to the shaping of all subsequent economic development. Politics in this sense of substructural social relationship and process is indeed central to our analysis, however often the state may seem absent, irrelevant, or uniform in its actions across partisan lines.

Our interpretations begin with a reevaluation of the colonial heritage and a correction of the long-standing focus on land tenure and the hacienda. We are convinced that land tenure (narrowly defined) and land scarcity are not the critical variables so often assumed to explain most or all of the region's modern history. Nearly everywhere in mid-nineteenth-century Central America land was in relative (and at times absolute) abundance, whereas capital (both material and human) and labor were lacking.[8] Thus, the productive systems that emerged everywhere reflected an attempt to solve a similar equation but with the most varied outcomes. Social and political struggle, some within the state and much outside, led to diverse outcomes, not the workings of any singular model or landlord power over land resources. Paradoxically, elite-commoner relationships (as often merchant-producer as land-lord-peasant relationships) *did* determine social change in the key period at midcentury but neither group was neatly arranged into partisan bands fighting for control of the state nor divided simply along patriarch-folk or landlord-peasant lines.

Access to land was important, at times critically so, but more important was access to credit, markets, transport, education, and political representation. Peasants in Nicaragua and Honduras had no difficulty in gaining access to land, but they virtually had no means of acquiring any of the latter weapons of self-defense. After the Liberal forces pushing for export growth succeeded in concentrating control over credit and political power, commoners in El Salvador and Guatemala found that access to land eventually could be denied them as well. After midcentury, a commoner population emerged in Costa Rica with access to credit, public lands, and education. Although in the twentieth century they were reduced to having microscopic properties little different from their Salvadoran brethren, the commoners had resources to overcome the political repression and disenfranchisement that swept over the region after 1930. We cite another, more prosaic element of class struggle rarely noted in the land-centric and state-centric interpretive framework: totally different results occurred when the universally regressive import-based tax structure and its revenues were used to support public education, road building, and lending, as was often the case in Costa Rica, than when the state supported programs of interest only to an elite that saw itself as both ruling and "owning" the future society. Such state choices are a clear illustration of the balance of power between different groups mentioned above.

The reevaluation of the colonial heritage and the foreshortening that results from giving a more central role to midcentury processes allow us to revisit Burns's influential interpretation of the nineteenth century. Within the Latin American historiographical context our position questions several aspects of his interpretation of Liberal triumph as stripping a largely homogeneous folk or peasant society of not only its communal land base but also its Conservative, patriarchal, or popular strongman protection.[9] We find that both Conservatives and caudillos were similar to Liberals in many key aspects. Their refusal to undo Liberal anticlerical policies from the 1840s on with regard to real property anticipated what would eventually become their common lands policy as well. Distinctions between folk and patriarch become more complex. Furthermore, attitudes toward ethnicity, land tenure, and the services that might be provided by the state also become more fluid and blurred.

Conservatives actually laid the groundwork for Liberal dispossessive measures, and they did so out of a similar commitment to export and state revenue growth, however ambiguous their view of a resulting "modernity" compared with the blatantly Europeanizing tastes of their Liberal opponents. For example, Conservative-appointed land survey-ors actually carried out many of the surveys that later Liberals would use to privatize ownership of formerly rented common lands in Guate-mala and elsewhere throughout the isthmus. Today their words may well sound naive at best, cynical at worst, when they insist that villagers must be made to see how, despite forced rentals to outsiders, no doubt exists as to permanent village ownership of the land.

Not surprisingly, the surveyors were directing their words to the arch-defender of the Central American folk, Rafael Carrera. For Burns this period was the folk's golden age because of Carrera's protection of the peasant and Indian masses. However, the same term was used by Luis Wolfram, the German immigrant land surveyor, to refer to the last years of the Carrera regime. In this case, however, Wolfram was fondly remembering the best years of his professional career when he fever-ishly surveyed forced rental lands for Conservative authorities.[10] After 1871, he continued his profession of measuring properties for freehold deeds under Liberal auspices, whose policies were much more to his ideological liking.

Beyond the issue of which elite faction is to be blamed or praised for

9

land privatization, the more important point is that key fissures had already appeared within folk society well before their erstwhile defenders, such as the Conservatives and strongmen (à la Carrera), vanished from the scene, and the divisions occurred in part because of the Conservatives' own policies. Within villager (and particularly, non-Indian villager) society many sought to and did participate in export, perennial production, and land privatization. Their appearance and strengthening before Liberal reform undoubtedly hastened the demise of Conservative rule because it added to the nonelite supporters of the Liberal agenda on land and the virtues of private property.

The essays that form this book have both informative or descriptive and interpretive or revisionist goals, and both goals involve potential readers in different ways. Thus, we need to explain how the essays and arguments are arranged and how they relate to one another. For the reader who is unfamiliar with Central America and its history we hope to provide both a basic introduction and a series of critical perspectives on the region in this period. Thus, we begin with a fairly detailed description of the region's economy at the beginning of its independent existence in 1821, along with the changes brought by independence itself. We then look at the major economic activities of the time, both for export and for local markets, and show how the gold rush and the increased commercial activity along the Pacific coast after midcentury represented a turning point for the economies of Central America. Here, as with the earlier discussion of colonial indigo production, we offer considerable descriptive detail, convinced as we are that no serious discussion of the economy, social organization, and politics is possible without the reader having a basic familiarity with the technical requirements and contemporary characteristics of major crops and productive activities. Here, too, we contrast coffee, that great engine of midcentury change, with other activities in terms of the demands it made on the institutional structure inherited from colonial times. In doing so we try to show the complex relationship between the form of incorporation into the world economy and specific policies and institutions. We then look at the ways in which this increasing reliance on export agriculture, in particular but not exclusively coffee, altered the market distribution and tax collection systems throughout the region.

In the second essay we offer a reinterpretation of the meaning of both the Liberal-Conservative conflict and many of the most conflictive political issues of the time. Building on the familiarity with the region's socioeconomic structure gained in the first essay, we offer a more speculative, interpretive, and at times polemical framework for understanding nineteenth-century politics and the meaning of the Liberal revolutions that were to follow after 1871. We discuss the presumptions and silences the partisan factions shared, more basic in fact than the postures and proclamations that so bitterly divided them, and we look at policy issues, such as common lands versus private ownership, the Church versus secularization, and equality versus hierarchy in class, gender, or ethnic terms, to show how much of both the best and the worst of the Liberal reform was readily visible well before 1871. In this effort we believe that even the introductory-level student of Central American history of this period will be served better by considering novel ways of thinking about "the facts" than by a recitation of them in a traditional, disingenuous narrative style.

In alternating between detailed description and interpretation we consciously have used the valuable insights of contemporary social theorists familiar with the region, in particular anthropologists, and are well aware of the dangers of anachronistic borrowing. We have also sought to retain some substantial flavor of the times by quoting extensively from both travelers' accounts and the often fiery rhetoric of political combatants. The reader whose curiosity has been piqued by these brief accounts will find more extensive citation and discussion of each of these kinds of sources, as well as primary and secondary materials for this period (wherever possible in their English editions), in Suggestions for Further Reading.

If our arguments are at times revisionist, they are so in two quite different ways. Some of the more extensive claims or critiques we may advance, especially regarding politics, land tenure conflicts, or the timing of export growth, will come as no surprise to fellow Latin Americanists unfamiliar with the peculiarities of Central America. However, fellow Central Americanists, long habituated to the dominant, Liberal-derived interpretive framework still so strong today in the region, may be startled. Similarly, certain peculiarities of Central America taken for granted by regional specialists—such oddities as the structure of regional economic specialization, the hyperabundance of land and scarcity of labor in the nineteenth century, or the kaleidoscope of ambiguous ethnic terminology—may come as something of a surprise to specialists on other regions.

This work explores ways of thinking about the changes that took

Introduction

place in Central America in the first half century of independent life and how they affected subsequent developments. The structure of the work is neither narrative nor simply descriptive. Rather, we hope to offer a series of critical perspectives on a period and region not well known by nonspecialists. Out of the supposed "archetype of anarchy," we seek to extract both coherence and significance. If such a seemingly quixotic attempt leads to further debate and discussion, our purpose will have been served.

Notes

1. The classic characterization made by Tulio Halperín Donghi in *Historia contemporánea de América Latina* (Madrid: Alianza Editorial, 1970).

2. Mario Rodríguez, *The Cádiz Experiment in Central America* (Berkeley: University of California Press, 1978).

3. E. Bradford Burns, *The Poverty of Progress: Latin America in the Nineteenth Century* (Berkeley: University of California Press, 1980).

4. For a careful analysis of the comparative data and a challenge to established wisdom on this point, see "El significado social de la Caficultura costarricense y salvadorena," in *El café en la historia agraria centroamericana,* ed. Mario Samper Kutschbach and Héctor Pérez Brignoli (San José, Costa Rica: FLACSO, 1994).

5. David Bushnell and Neil Macaulay, *The Emergence of Latin America in the Nineteenth Century* (New York: Oxford University Press, 1988), chap. 8, passim.

6. Florencia E. Mallon, "Economic Liberalism: Where We Are and Where We Need to Go," in *Guiding the Invisible Hand*, ed. Joseph Love and Nils Jacobsen (New York: Praeger, 1988), 179.

7. Theda Skocpol et al., eds., *Bringing the State Back In* (London: Cambridge University Press, 1985).

8. A concise statement of the landlord-based political model for understanding Central America can be found in John Weeks, "An Interpretation of the Central American Crisis," *Latin American Research Review* 21 (1986): 31–54.

9. Burns, *The Poverty of Progress*; and *Patriarch and Folk: The Emergence of Modern Nicaragua, 1798–1858* (Cambridge: Harvard University Press, 1991).

10. "Under the Carrera administration the beneficent laws of Gálvez [1830s Liberal decrees privatizing land] daily developed further, multiplying the number of private properties in the *ejidos* [lands given to towns] of the Indian population. . . . When we arrived (in early 1862) . . . the country under that conservative and parsimonious system gave signs of a real golden age." Luis Wolfram, *Principios elementales de la economía social sobre la civilización de los pueblos y los progresos de la agricultura* (Guatemala: Tipografía La Estrella, 1887), 38–39.

The Economy of Central America

From Bourbon Reforms to Liberal Reforms

Héctor Lindo-Fuentes

The rapid increase in agricultural exports that took place in the nine-teenth century left an indelible mark on the economies and societies of Central American countries. On this issue, at least, agreement exists. A useful way to look at the economic transformations of the nineteenth century is through the prism of their legacy, and our attention should be directed primarily to the study of the impact of exports on the formation of the society and the state. For Héctor Pérez Brignoli the expansion of coffee cultivation that characterized the period "introduced fundamental structural changes in land markets, labor relations, business, and financial organization."[1] Victor Bulmer-Thomas agrees with the substance of this interpretation when he says that the rapid growth in exports in the half century that preceded 1920 "transformed the region's social relations. The traditional élite, consisting of a small merchant class and landowners with extensive cattle interests, began to be replaced by a powerful group associated with the export sector either as growers, traders or financiers."[2]

Until recently, the widespread consensus on the impact of exports on Central America was facilitated by the lack of knowledge of exactly what happened in Central America during the nineteenth century. Recent research has begun to explore exactly when and how that rapid export growth took place and how the fundamental changes mentioned by Pérez Brignoli were introduced. This comparative essay, possible because of recent historiographical developments, shows how the change in direction of the Central American economies was not, as commonly believed, the result of the Liberal reforms of the 1870s; the change began decades earlier and gathered speed after the opening of the Panama Railroad in 1855.

The Economy

The expansion of these economies did not take place in a vacuum but rather in the shadow of a preexisting system. It is important to understand the tools available to the new countries that were used to adapt to the new realities. Thus, the point of departure for this essay will be a brief discussion of those aspects of the colonial heritage that had a direct impact on the economy. We are interested in the relationship between resources inherited from the colonial period and the needs imposed by the rapid growth of export agriculture in the second half of the century. Our aim is to explore how this interaction between external stimulus and internal response, between the legacy of the past and the promise of the future, gave a specific character to each country of the isthmus.

The Colonial Heritage

The first step in understanding the economic transformations is to discuss the meaning of the colonial legacy in light of its reaction to the pressure of export agriculture. The idea is widely accepted that, from the economic point of view, the foremost colonial heritage in Latin America was the hacienda. One of the better known statements of this idea was given by Stanley and Barbara Stein: "The most significant heritage of Iberian colonialism was the tradition of the large estate, producing food-stuffs and raw materials for local consumption or for export to Western Europe. . . . It represented a type of social organization, a source of social prestige and political power as well as wealth and income. . . . Until the twentieth century, the basis of oligarchy in Latin America has been the monopolization of, and access to, land ownership."[3]

Our first task will be to put this notion aside, at least for the Central American case. There, among all factors of production (capital, labor, land, and entrepreneurship), land was by far the most abundant. The economic role of land and the hacienda, important as it was, deserves conceptual refinement. How could the control of the most abundant factor be the key to wealth? The haciendas were much more than simply landownership. They were economic units where all the factors of production were organized to carry out a productive activity; what mattered was the ability to acquire and organize all the factors. The hacienda was the physical location of those activities, but to identify wealth with land is a conceptual mistake. Other forms of landownership (*ejidos* and communal lands) existed where the same economic activities were carried out with greater or lesser success. (Ejidos were lands given to towns to use for grazing and

14

agriculture; they belonged to the town, and their use depended on permissions issued by town authorities.) In addition, vast expanses of unclaimed lands owned by the crown (*tierras realengas*) existed. Given its relative abundance, land was not the most difficult factor to acquire. Entrepreneurial ability, credit, and labor were, in that order, the scarcest factors. It is not surprising, then, to observe that during the colonial period the biggest fortunes were made by such Guatemalan merchants as the marquis of Aycinena who, taking advantage of the regulations and privileges that derived from Spanish colonial policies, had the greatest capacity to organize complex economic activities that were the main source of credit. Notably, it was much easier to start as a merchant and end up owning land than the other way around. (It is difficult to talk about merchants or producers in an abstract sense; one of the characteristics of the economic life of the period was the limited division of labor, which means that for some individuals the main occupation was commerce and for others it was agricultural production.)

Of course, our discussion should not be limited to a comparison of production factors. The colonial regime implied a series of regulations that guaranteed unequal access to each factor. The limited educational system reduced the universe from which successful entrepreneurs could arise. Trade restrictions left international commerce (the main source of capital accumulation) in the hands of Spaniards and Creoles. Moreover, the essence of the colonial situation defined the Indian population as labor, and labor-recruiting practices were often violent and compulsory. Finally, access to land was determined by colonial regulations that created a mosaic of units with different legal statuses alongside vast amounts of tierras realengas. This situation created a clear division in society where the ethnic dimension and the links to colonial authorities carried great weight.

The commercial restrictions that were in effect during most of the colonial period had another notable consequence: they determined the destination of exports and the transportation network (limited as it was). Two outlets were used for the products of the region. The outlet on the Atlantic side was the Golfo Dulce, which opened to the Gulf of Honduras and was the locus for the commercial activity controlled by the Guatemalan merchants. They primarily controlled the exports of Guatemala, El Salvador, and Honduras. The southern countries more easily escaped the control of these merchants and the colonial authorities and often directed their limited trade to the contraband market via the San Juan River or via Panama and South America.

The Economy

Economic activity was limited by more than the endowment of factors of production and the transportation network. Total demand was small. With most of the population living barely above subsistence levels and with low productivity, internal markets were limited. The export sector faced the constraint of extremely high transportation costs because exports produced on the Pacific coast had to be exported to European markets located on the other side of the Atlantic. The small size of the external sector was, then, the result of something more than colonial restrictions. Nevertheless, because of colonial restrictions and power relationships, the indigo trade, the main link with the outside world (even if a small percentage of overall economic activity), cast a long shadow over the rest of the economy.

Indigo Production and Trade

At the beginning of the nineteenth century, besides the small group of people dedicated to trade, small crafts, and the civil and military bureaucracy, most Central Americans were devoted to subsistence agriculture. Export agriculture, in contrast, was a relatively small part of economic activity. Nonetheless, it is worth analyzing it in detail because it represented the main source of income for the colonial elite and, as time passed, was the basis for the most dynamic sector of the economy. Indigo was the main commercial link with the metropolis. Its production and commercialization represented the most complex economic activity of the colony, and its producers and merchants were the most influential citizens. Indeed, the commercialization of indigo was the springboard for a small group to exert control over trade relationships throughout the colony.

A brief discussion of indigo's cultivation, processing, and commercialization exemplifies three characteristics of the colonial period: the persistence of traditional agricultural techniques that remained unchanged for centuries, the impact of commercial agriculture on labor, and the key role played by credit and commercial contacts for the Guatemalan merchant elite to appropriate most of its benefits. This latter point needs to be emphasized because the example of indigo illustrates how the control of trade and credit mechanisms was more of a key to economic power than mere landownership.

Although the area where *jiquilite* (the plant from which indigo was extracted) was grown ranged from western Guatemala to the coast of Lake Nicaragua, most production occurred in El Salvador. Descriptions of its

16

Indigo obraje *in Nicaragua, 1855*
(*from* Harper's New Monthly Magazine, *November 1855*)

cultivation and processing in the eighteenth century differ little from similar descriptions written a century earlier. The eighteenth-century description of the method of cultivation is as follows. Land was cleared in January and February. In March the land was torched, and the seed was broadcast for it to spring with the April rains. With the arrival of May the weeding began and lasted until June. The procedure was repeated at the end of August or early September. Later that month or in October the plants were harvested and processed.

Heavy bundles of jiquilite branches were brought to the indigo works (*obrajes*) for processing. The extraction of the dye was carried out in two brick vats placed next to each other at different heights. The harvested leaves were placed in water in the higher vat. After ten or twelve hours, when the leaves were sufficiently decomposed (the fermentation point could be recognized because the liquid turned a light green), the mix was passed to the second vat. Once the mix was in the second vat, a paddle wheel operated manually or by animals constantly stirred the water until its color changed first to light blue and then to a deeper shade. The shade indicated the saturation point (*punto*), that is, when the concentration of indigo reached its maximum, a determination made by the *puntero* (the individual in charge of identifying the saturation point [*punto*], at which time the water had to be drained). Once the puntero was satisfied with the shade of blue, he stopped the wheel. When the water was still, a blue sediment slowly settled at the bottom of the vat, and the water recovered its natural transparency. At the end of this stage the water was drained, and the sediment was put to dry in cone-shaped cotton strainers. The dry indigo was wrapped in straw mats (*petates*) and packed in the 150-pound leather bags (*zurrones*) used to ship it to market.

No barriers to entry that would lead to a monopolistic structure were created by the knowledge needed to carry out these activities (transmitted by tradition), the capital investment (simple brick structures), or the labor demands (limited to harvest time). On the contrary, small producers (*poquiteros*) used a slightly different and more elaborate processing technique that yielded the highest quality indigo. In fact, up until the end of the nineteenth century the small producers played an important role in total production.

Labor shortages occurred during harvest time, so landowners, in complicity with the authorities, used tricks to obtain labor. By the end of the colonial period the *repartimiento* (the coercive labor system whereby for a few weeks every year the Indian towns had to provide a certain amount of labor to work on roads and haciendas), debt peonage, and wage labor were the principal means of obtaining labor for commercial agriculture. Labor shortages were such that, by the end of the eighteenth century, the crown authorized the repartimiento of mestizos, mulattoes, sambos, and blacks to work in indigo obrajes. Although the Cortes de Cádiz abolished all forms of compulsory labor, the practice of repartimiento, together with debt peonage, continued. Following long-established colonial traditions, local economic imperatives proved more powerful than laws passed by distant authorities.

According to the instructions of the deputy of the Kingdom of Guatemala to the Cortes de Cádiz, indigo was "nearly the only product that sustains the commercial relations with the metropolis."[4] The main distribution networks were organized around its trade, with the Guatemalan merchants serving as arbiters. They constituted, in Troy Floyd's words, "a monopoly comprised of a phalanx of Creoles and peninsulars, closely knit by ties of marriage, blood, and commercial interest."[5] The power of the merchants stemmed from their links with commercial houses in Spain (who bought the dye and, in exchange, sold manufactures), their role as providers of credit, and their ability to create a system practically unassailable by their competitors. The system worked more or less as follows. The small indigo producers took their product to the local fairs if they could transport it and, if not, sold it to intermediaries or to big producers who had access to mules. The most important buyers at the fairs were the big producers who owned mule trains to make the trip to the great annual fair in Guatemala, where the Guatemalan merchants waited, ready to play their triple role as indigo exporters, importers of European manufactures, and money lenders. The producers, after endless bargaining, left the fair with loans in money or in local or imported products, all received from the merchants, and on arrival in their localities became distributors selling in local fairs or placing the merchandise through third parties. Through this process the fate of the Guatemalan merchants was intimately linked to that of the producers of El Salvador, Nicaragua, and Honduras, and the fairs were the stage for the most important commercial transactions.

Controlling credit also permitted merchants to control the commercial activity generated by the *repartimiento de bienes* (the method used by Spanish authorities to force Indians to buy goods). The *alcaldes mayores* (the colonial authorities who had jurisdiction over districts of the Captaincy General of Guatemala), who needed substantial sums as deposit or bond demanded by the colonial authorities, received an advance from the merchant. The alcalde mayor's objective was far from innocent. The alcalde mayor was committed to distribute merchandise, thus starting the cycle of repartimiento de bienes.

The system led to much friction; the relationship between indigo producers and merchants, for example, was rocky. The former had countless complaints against the latter, who used their economic and political power as leverage in discussions on prices or credit terms. To mediate in these conflicts the colonial authorities made intermittent efforts to regulate indigo prices and decreed the creation of the Montepío de Cosecheros de Añil (Indigo Growers Credit Society), an institution designed to compete with merchants in the credit market.

For economic and political reasons it was difficult to confront the power of the merchants. After all, because of their contacts in Spain they held the key to trade with Europe, and because of the ability to extend credit they could control internal distribution networks. Some of these merchants were skillful peninsular businessmen who had seen the commercial possibilities of indigo and had settled in Guatemala, where they rapidly established links with the oldest and most prominent families of the capital. In sum, they had the knowledge of commercial practices on both sides of the Atlantic, a rare skill in the colony.

The main participants in this exchange were the Guatemalans and the Salvadorans. Hondurans and Nicaraguans participated to a lesser degree, with some indigo or with cattle sold in the fairs to provide meat or hides to manufacture zurrones. The link between internal markets and the indigo trade, created by peculiar credit practices that will be discussed in the next section, allowed markets to have a reach that, given the transportation difficulties, would not have been possible otherwise. The profit margin of indigo, a product with high value per unit of volume, allowed it to absorb the high transportation costs, which explains why producers were willing to make the long trips to Guatemala from Honduras or El Salvador. In addition, on their way back from Guatemala, these producers carried imported products and local crafts that by themselves would not have justified the trip. Costa Rica's links with the indigo economy were weaker, although it engaged in the regional trade of tobacco and cattle. Costa Rica and Nicaragua, given the geographic location of both countries, had their natural trading partners in the south and did engage in legal and illegal trade with South American markets. Not surprisingly, the Guatemalan merchants fought that trade every step of the way. Costa Rica's imports from Panama were embargoed on a number of occasions as a result of explicit pressure coming from the Guatemalan merchants and their agents in León.

The logic of the commercial networks of Central America stemmed, then, from the colonial system: from the regulations that provided privileges to those with commercial connections in Cádiz, from tax policies that forced Indians to participate in the market, and from the role of the alcaldes mayores. When that logic disappeared after 1821, the commercial networks of the colonial period were condemned to extinction.

Credit

An essential part of the monopoly power of the Guatemalan merchants was the scarcity of credit. The main form of credit was the *habilitación*, a loan made partially in silver and partially in merchandise. The loan was to be paid in agricultural products at the end of the year. As described earlier, in his role as provincial merchant the indigo producer received merchandise and money and contracted the obligation to pay the following year with the indigo crop. The nominal interest of 5 percent was in fact much higher because the wholesaler received the indigo at prices negotiated in his favor and gave merchandise at the prices he found most convenient. The habilitación system was repeated at the different commercial levels. This system was the credit hierarchy, which began with such transactions as the one just described between wholesalers and retailers in the capital and in the provinces. The retailers, in turn, granted credit to small retailers and peddlers who took the merchandise to the far corners of the colony. At the provincial level a version of the system existed whereby the alcaldes mayores functioned as agents of the Guatemalan merchants and granted habilitaciones to indigo producers.

Complementing the Guatemalan merchants were two other sources of credit: the Church and the Montepío de Cosecheros de Añil. Limited as they were, these credit sources were in a deep crisis by the end of the colonial period. Two events had contributed to weaken the credit system, and both were related to the conflicts between Spain and England that resulted from the two treaties of San Ildefonso between Charles IV and postrevolutionary France. First, the conflict between Spain and England interrupted trade; between 1798 and 1802 the indigo crops had to be stored in warehouses until trade was reestablished. Second, to finance his disastrous alliance with Napoleon, Charles IV and Godoy, his minister, decided in 1804 to extend to the colonies the debt consolidation that had already taken place in Spain. This consolidation consisted of the sale of real estate of the *obras pías* (church charities such as *capellanías* [the institution whereby interest produced by a property was designated to pay for religious services], convents, monasteries, hospitals, schools, and Indian and Ladino *cofradías* [lay religious brotherhoods; they often owned property whose products paid for religious services]), the product of which was deposited in the royal treasury. The crown committed itself to pay the owners 5 percent interest on the deposits. The whole affair severely damaged the credit-granting capacity of the Church and the cofradías. The Montepío, which was just another link in the credit chain, was a victim of the same pressures. Its main debtors, the indigo producers, could not pay their debts. Facing bad years, with their money frozen in indigo bales warehoused in Veracruz, the producers had to pay their debts to the obras pías all at once. The situation was so precarious that when independence arrived the interest payments on the average loan of the Montepío had not been made for seven years.

It is no exaggeration to say that when independence arrived the traditional credit sources were in crisis. The Guatemalan merchants, who had contributed to the European wars with "patriotic donations," faced the growing competition of British merchants on the Atlantic coast, the Church had become a victim of debt consolidation, and the Montepío was bankrupt.

Labor

Access to labor was directly related to the social stratification established by the colonial regime, but it was not the only variable. First, clear differences in population density existed in the various regions, which reflected rather closely the strengths of the links with the metropolis. El Salvador and Guatemala, the centers of indigo production and distribution, had the greatest population density and the most powerful elites. The former had almost twelve inhabitants per square kilometer, and the latter had about five and one-half inhabitants per square kilometer. In the rest of the isthmus population density did not reach two inhabitants per square kilometer (see Table 1). The differences, by the way, are great enough to overcome the imperfections of the data of the period and are confirmed by qualitative evidence.

In addition, clear differences existed in the distribution of the population within each state of the future federation. In Honduras, already an underpopulated area, the eastern provinces were nearly empty, and the population was scattered in the central and western zones in settlements isolated by the difficulties of a mountainous geography. In El Salvador, the distribution was more even, although almost half of the population lived in the central zone; significant numbers of people lived around Sonsonate, Santa Ana, and San Miguel. In Nicaragua most people lived between the lakes and the Pacific, and in Costa Rica most people lived in the small towns of the Central Valley. Finally, in Guatemala the population was concentrated in the area surrounding the capital. In general terms it could be said that Central Americans preferred the fertile valleys close to the Pacific Ocean and that the main settlements were in the northeastern part of the isthmus.

As we have seen, population concentrated where export agriculture was most important. Labor was in high demand and compulsory labor recruitment was most frequent in this area. Compulsory labor recruitment practices were deeply rooted in the colonial situation; they were a product

The Colonial Heritage

Table 1. Central America's Estimated Population ca. 1820

Country	Population	Population per square kilometer
Costa Rica	63,000	1.2
El Salvador	248,000	11.9
Guatemala	595,000	5.5
Honduras	135,000	1.2
Nicaragua	186,000	1.3
Central America	1,227,000	2.8

Source: Ralph Lee Woodward, Jr., "Central America," in *Spanish America after Independence, c. 1820–c. 1870,* ed. Leslie Bethell (Cambridge: Cambridge University Press, 1987), 178.

of the relationships between the dominant and the dominated. The repartimiento, the tribute, certain forms of *encomienda* (the Indian group given to a Spaniard; the Spaniard received labor and tribute and in exchange was supposed to provide a Christian education), debt peonage, and *colonato* (the institution whereby laborers [*colonos*], in exchange for their labor, were allowed to live on the estate and were given plots to cultivate land with subsistence products) operated through mechanisms established to control the Indian population. Labor recruitment took place in Indian towns with the cooperation of *corregidores* (authorities in Indian towns) and alcaldes (who in turn were frequently of noble Indian background, which gave them authority within their communities). In this fashion the relative importance of the Indian population and the persistence of its organization according to colonial patterns contributed to the permanence of compulsory forms of labor recruitment that, in turn, were more likely to occur where the prosperity of commercial agriculture created labor demands.

Although it is impossible to obtain precise data on the relative importance of the Indian population at the end of the colonial period, no doubt exists that the largest number of Indians lived in Guatemala (in 1770 about 68 percent of the tributaries of the Captaincy General lived in Guatemala) and the smallest number lived in Costa Rica (less than 1 percent of tributaries in 1770). Considerable differences existed even in the two countries with the greatest population density. By the end of the colonial period in El Salvador, Honduras, and Nicaragua, the process of "ladinization" (acculturation to Spanish ways, which sometimes were combined with miscegenation) was well advanced, whereas in Guatemala most of the Indian population kept its language and customs.

Thus, by the end of the colonial period the presence of export agriculture and the abundance of Indians in Guatemala gave this country conditions for a more generalized persistence of compulsory labor recruitment. Hence, Guatemala was the country where, decades later, the demands imposed by the expansion of coffee cultivation put greater pressure on the labor markets and where the heaviest burdens were imposed on the Indian population.

As this discussion illustrates, the use of compulsory labor recruitment gained importance in the presence of export agriculture, and it was more frequent in Guatemala and El Salvador than in the rest of Central America. The Costa Rican case was at the opposite end of the spectrum. There the scarcity of labor, the slight importance of export agriculture, and the prevalence of Creoles and Ladinos in the total population resulted in the expansion of small property in the Central Valley, the use of wage labor, and a limited number of slaves in cattle haciendas.

Land

It is worth stressing that export agriculture was not the main occupation for most of the population. The main economic activities were agriculture and cattle raising to satisfy the needs of an economy that Adriaan Van Oss rightly called "self-sufficient."[6] These activities were carried out with land, the access to which was regulated according to three principal forms that evolved throughout the colonial period: (1) the haciendas, more or less direct heirs of the royal land grants and the *composiciones* (mechanism for claiming land); (2) the ejidos, lands given to Ladino towns for planting crops; and (3) the communal lands given to Indian towns. Other land included large expanses of unclaimed territory that belonged to the Crown, the tierras realengas, renamed with the more republican term *terrenos baldíos* (unclaimed land owned by the state) after independence. The Church, on the other hand, owned vast amounts of land, mainly in Guatemala. Nonetheless, before the export growth that took place in the second half of the nineteenth century, competition for land, given the lack of demographic density, was limited to land surrounding towns or particularly apt for commercial agriculture (fertile and with easy access).

The characteristics that had the most impact were the variety of land tenure arrangements, the uncertainty that resulted from ill-defined property boundaries and deeds, and the geographical location of population settlements, which did not necessarily coincide with the areas where commercial agriculture expanded during the second half of the nineteenth century. The confusion surrounding land tenure and the lack of clarity in deeds had been a constant source of friction during the colonial period and became an even greater problem when commercial agriculture expanded. Because the creation of coffee plantations involved long-term investment (coffee trees take at least four years to start producing), it made no sense to invest in them without a clear deed. Moreover, it was impossible to develop a credit system based on mortgages if landownership was less than secure.

The last point, that of the location of settlements, influenced both access to labor and competition regarding land. In Guatemala, for example, Indian communities were located in areas far from coffee plantations, which created difficulties in the recruitment of labor but allowed Indian towns to keep and even augment their lands, at least during the period under consideration. In El Salvador the situation was different because the lands appropriate for coffee cultivation frequently coincided with the location of ejidos and communal lands. In this case a slow process of erosion of Indian property occurred, which was furthered by the Liberal reforms of the 1880s. In Costa Rica the population was, from the beginning, concentrated in settlements in the Central Valley, an ideal zone for the cultivation of coffee because of the relatively easy access to the Pacific coast and because of abundant land. Given these characteristics, the problem that arose with commercial agriculture was not one of competition for land but the expansion of the agricultural frontier. Thus, with regard to land, the colonial heritage in Central America was not the hacienda but rather the interaction between different forms of property ownership, settlement patterns, and labor needs.

Internal Markets and Trade Routes

The economy was to a great extent closed to the outside world; internal trade, in contrast, was vibrant, with all segments of the population participating in it. An active trade in food and small crafts existed that was based on the production of crafts by members of the Indian and Ladino communities. The modesty of the crafts does not diminish their importance; people devoted a good part of their energies to production and distribution. Because labor-intensive artisanal techniques were used, the time devoted to the production of textiles, ceramic items, and basketry was considerable.

Not even the simplest innovations of the industrial revolution had reached the textile industry. In the absence of gins, cotton was cleaned by beating it with two wooden sticks that loosened the fiber and released the black seeds and other impurities. This process was conducted over a leather cushion stuffed with corn husks. Spinning was equally simple; Indian women sat on the ground with a lump of newly cleaned cotton on their laps and spent long hours spinning a simple wooden stick that rested on a wooden or ceramic bowl. Brilliant colors appealed to consumers, and the extraction of the dyes used to color the thread was a labor-intensive task. All dyes, whether the purple extracted from mollusks, the blue from indigo, the black from shells, or the yellow from campeche, required a long and cumbersome process of extraction. Hand looms were no different from those observed in pre-Columbian Mayan figurines. José Cecilio del Valle, the statesman and author of the act of independence, estimated that by the end of the eighteenth century in Guatemala a thousand looms had to be supplied with thread.[7] Each artisanal activity required a similar variety of simple and time-consuming steps. The economy was certainly self-sufficient, and the people were devoted to subsistence activities, but these simple terms obscure the number and variety of tasks that occupied the daily life of the population at large.

A good deal of the diligence of the Indians in participating in the market was due to the obligations imposed by the tribute and the repartimiento de bienes that forced them to participate in the money economy. In textile production, in particular, the repartimiento de bienes played an important role. The textile industry was structured around the peculiarities of the colonial system. Essential for its functioning was the ability of merchants to use the coercive apparatus of the state and take advantage of trade restrictions. Besides textiles, Guatemalan Indians produced earthenware, nets, ropes, and straw mats; they cultivated achiote, sarsaparilla, copal, sugarcane, cacao, wheat, vegetables, pepper; and they extracted salt and lead. All products were sold at local and regional markets.

Internal markets, usually small, were arranged around inefficient and unfair regulations that gave great advantage to a few merchants and forced many to work for little compensation. The access to external markets, on the other hand, was limited by geography and even more regulations. The main obstacle to transporting colonial products to the European markets was not the Atlantic Ocean but bringing them to the coast. The most productive agricultural areas were located close to the Pacific and were separated from the Atlantic by a wall of mountains. Bringing products to the ports represented the greatest percentage of transportation costs. In bad years, when buccaneers or direct attacks from foreign powers added an element of danger to trade through the Gulf of Honduras, it was necessary to send mule trains loaded with merchandise all the way to Veracruz.

By the late eighteenth century Guatemala's main outlets to the Atlantic were Izabal, which had replaced the Bodegas del Golfo Dulce in 1803, and Santo Tomás. In northern Honduras, Omoa and Trujillo were to a large extent occupied with contraband. Nicaragua had access to the Atlantic through San Juan del Norte, which received goods from the agricultural zone of Granada via the San Juan River and Lake Nicaragua. The northern coast of Costa Rica was serviced by the port of Matina. The activity on the Pacific ports was still marginal. Every year Acajutla, on the coast of El Salvador, Realejo in Nicaragua, and Puntarenas in Costa Rica were visited by two or three ships carrying trade to Quito or Valparaíso. Smaller boats were active in the trade between Puntarenas and Panama, although the absolute amounts of the merchandise moved was limited. Overland transportation was conducted mainly by mule trains that moved over difficult trails that were dusty in the dry months and muddy and badly eroded during the rainy season. High transportation costs worked against the integration of Central American markets. Yet, the organization imposed by Guatemalan merchants allowed the achievement of a certain level of integration, but the colonial regulations that gave them special leverage were bound to disappear, thus removing the glue that had integrated those markets.

As the three centuries of colonial rule were coming to an end, a form of organizing the economy had evolved. Institutions and interactions shaped by the nature of colonialism varied in time and space. Local conditions determined which institutions of the colonial repertoire would be used and how they would be adapted. The industrial and French revolutions and the Napoleonic wars provided stimulus for change. Mercantilistic trade regulations and colonial power relationships helped a small group of merchants to exercise great control over credit. This structure would prove to be one of the most fragile bequests of the colonial period because credit

The Economy

Traveling in Guatemala, ca. 1839 (from Incidents of Travel in Central America, Chiapas and Yucatán *[New York: 1841])*

arrangements were dependent on the existence of a metropolis with the capacity to enforce its commercial regulations. As that capacity weakened so did the strength of the credit structure. The crisis of the years that preceded independence delivered serious blows to the Church and to the Montepío; the role of the Guatemalan merchants waned when English merchants and Belizean commercial houses began to take advantage of Spanish weaknesses even before independence. The organization of the scarce labor force, in contrast, was based on social relationships that could not be removed by the mere fact of independence. Labor was often organized with coercive methods that, true to their colonial origin, were stronger when an Indian population was organized around towns and were more tempting where export agriculture increased demand for labor services. Thus, in Guatemala, where Indian groups were a significant percentage of the population, the repartimiento was more likely to survive (with changes) after independence, whereas in Costa Rica it was destined to disappear more easily. Paradoxically, the abundance of land left a troublesome legacy. The role of landownership was much more complex than what is suggested by stressing the importance of the hacienda as the nucleus of economic activity. The variety of land tenure arrangements and the uneven settlement pattern created an institutional environment full of ambiguities and ill-defined physical and legal boundaries. The redefinition

28

of those boundaries and the changing character of landed property were destined to constitute an arena for power struggles once export agriculture began to expand.

The definition of what was to be produced, and for whom, was also in a state of flux. Although much of the economic activity was directed toward subsistence products for local markets and although international trade, still a secondary pursuit, was undergoing a crisis, growing international demands and incipient trade liberalization suggested directions for the future.

From Traditional to Export Agriculture

The Consequences of Independence

Spain's changing political fortunes following the French Revolution weakened the legitimacy of its power. By 1821, local leaders were confronted with another swing in Spain's political roller coaster: an officers' revolt restoring the liberal Cádiz constitution. Leaders in the city of Guatemala decided to take their cues from Iturbide's conservative independence movement in Mexico. The effort in Guatemala was an attempt to change to ensure that things would remain the same, but control of events was beyond the leaders' reach.

The power of the Guatemalans weakened as the commercial network woven around the habilitación system began to unravel and as the credit offered by the Belizean merchants became more widely available. Trade relations were liberalized, and their direction began to change. From the convocation of the 1823–1824 Constitutional Assembly onward, the laws of the federation and of the different states followed the main lines of economic liberalism. Unforeseen circumstances contributed to the liberalization of trade, and the disorganization of the bureaucratic apparatus that followed independence encouraged tax evasion. Therefore, tax revenues fell regardless of the intentions of the new authorities. The impact of the liberalization of international trade was soon felt. The market was inundated with cheap imports, benefiting consumers at the same time they hurt the production of local artisans, particularly in the textile industry. José Cecilio del Valle estimated that only one hundred of the one thousand looms that existed in Guatemala could survive the competition of the new imports.[8] Manuel Montúfar summarized the impact of these changes on

29

industry when he commented that the old commercial system "began to suffer mortal blows, either from some monopolized foreign imports, or from clandestine ones, which greatly increased from then on, particularly through the British settlement of Belize on the coast of Honduras, which has absorbed, unnoticed, the wealth of Guatemala, and, as a result, industry has experienced a setback instead of improving."[9]

Inexpensive imports appealed to the general public but damaged artisans; low taxes stimulated trade but lowered fiscal revenue. These contradictory forces caused frequent changes in customs laws and tariffs and in the mix of internal taxes. A constant feature of this period was the distance between the letter of the law and its actual application. Both at the federation level and in the states the mechanisms to enforce economic legislation and to control contraband were weakened. The end result was a virtual laissez faire, a more radical change than any authority had in mind.

The positive economic stimulus provided by freer trade and more sources of credit was offset by an environment of political instability that hampered investment. The period of the federation was notorious for the tension between the states, which culminated in the fragmentation of Central America into five different countries. The list of battles prepared by the nineteenth-century historian Alejandro Marure is well known.[10] According to Marure, between 1824 and 1842 the army of the state of Guatemala participated in fifty-one battles, El Salvador participated in forty, Honduras fought in twenty-seven, and Costa Rica fought in five. These figures give an idea of the armed activity of the period, although they do not take into account the conflicts within each state. Undoubtedly this instability had a great impact on the economy. The wars often destroyed physical structures such as government buildings and indigo obrajes. The climate of instability negatively affected the incentive to invest. The uncertainty about the profitability of any venture was accompanied by the certainty of forced loans extracted by local caudillos. In addition to the investment difficulties were the problems created because the armies employed men in the prime age groups. Furthermore, during the wars it was difficult to find laborers because those who were not fighting went into hiding to avoid forced recruitment. Even when production was successful roads were dangerous, and bringing goods to the market was difficult. Thus, during the years of the federation the disruptions of investment, labor, and commercial activities delayed the growth of the economy.

Does this mean that the period of the federation coincided with what

Tulio Halperín Donghi called the long wait? To a point it did, but the negative impact of instability was not uniform either in time or space. Under Gálvez, Guatemala was stable enough for cochineal production to prosper. Costa Rica, because of its geographical position and relative lack of importance, was insulated from most wars and had a head start in coffee production. In Honduras the geographical dispersion of economic activity muffled the impact of the wars. In El Salvador and Nicaragua, on the contrary, the negative impact of the wars was more persistent. Most travelers who visited the region commented on the visible destruction and economic decadence there.

Despite the destruction, and partially because of it, creative forces were at play. Trends that were to dominate the economy in the future began to take shape. The political disintegration of Central America and the loss of the cohesive power of the credit of the Guatemalan merchants contributed to weakening the integration of the regional economies and, with the liberalization of external trade, to reorienting productive activity toward exports. Both trends can be observed in the direction of the roads built after the 1840s. As discussed later, when the new countries were able to pay attention to public works, the first priority was to build roads from the centers of production to the ports, while the old *camino real*, the inland road that linked the five states of the old federation, was allowed to deteriorate.

Once the political situation stabilized after the breakup of the federation, by far the most important change in the economy was its reorientation toward export agriculture. In the past, indigo production had been important for the ruling elite, but from a more general point of view the foremost economic activity during the colonial period was subsistence agriculture.

The speed and degree of the reorientation of the economies depended on the investment climate, the transportation costs, and the availability of alternatives. In the country most isolated from economic instability and, as a result, with a better investment climate (Costa Rica), the expansion of export agriculture was easier than in countries where instability was rampant (Nicaragua and El Salvador). At the same time, where geography made it difficult to improve transportation (Honduras) or where alternative export products existed (gold and silver in Honduras and precious woods in Nicaragua), export agriculture developed more slowly. Intermediate cases, such as Guatemala and El Salvador, confirm this picture; when they recovered their stability both countries experienced a clear change in

31

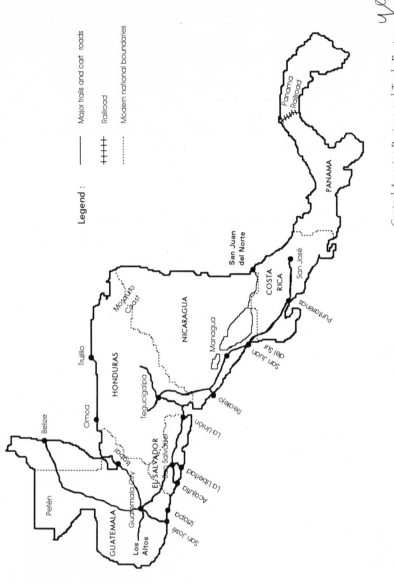

Central America Regions and Trade Routes

Legend :

⎯⎯⎯ Major trails and cart roads

⊢⊢⊢⊢ Railroad

·········· Modern national boundaries

GUATEMALA

Petén

Belize

Los Altos

Guatemala City

San José

Iztapa

EL SALVADOR

San Salvador

Acajutla

La Libertad

San José

Izabal

Omoa

Trujillo

HONDURAS

Mosquito Coast

Tegucigalpa

La Unión

Realejo

NICARAGUA

Managua

San Juan del Sur

San Juan del Norte

COSTA RICA

Puntarenas

San José

PANAMA

Panama Railroad

the investment climate and modified their production structure without losing sight of the profitability of alternative products (cochineal, indigo, and coffee). Following is a detailed discussion of the evolution of the investment climate, transportation costs, and alternative products. |

The Investment Climate

The turbulent 1820s and 1830s did much to break the hold of the credit system used by Guatemalan merchants as a means to control Central American trade, and political instability created a hostile environment for investors and delayed the development of new credit institutions‖ The limited credit that survived remained linked to trade. In 1825, G. A. Thompson, a British envoy, noted: "The most respectable families think it no degradation to be engaged in trade: as there is no bank and no interest for money, this is the only way in which they can employ their capitals. Most of the richer classes of inhabitants derive their incomes from the cattle bred upon their estates and their crops of indigo, cochineal and tobacco, which they barter with the European merchants for dry goods; retailing the latter for the consumption of the natives."[11]

This combination of trade and credit, not much different from colonial practices, remained in effect until the foundation of the first banks and beyond. The habilitaciones of this period were discussed in 1855 by a British *Board of Trade* pamphlet:

> Business is carried on by the importers in the following manner, viz.: they sell to resident merchants at about 80 per cent. upon invoice prices, payable in 12 months, either in part cash, part indigo, or all in indigo, at the current price of that article at the time the payment becomes due, or its market value at the time of purchase. These again dole out small invoices to the smaller shop-keepers, also upon long credits, and so every business is done upon trust; a cash sale of 3,000 dollars being seldom heard of.[12]

| Despite high interest rates, this kind of one-year credit was essential for the functioning of economic activities. It was said that no Central American producer or merchant was free of debts. The habilitación system was used all over Central America with few variations and in diverse activities. In Guatemala the production of cochineal was financed with advances from export houses. In Nicaragua, again, one-year advances were the main source of credit. For reasons that had more to do with risk and transaction

costs than with credit scarcity, interest rates remained high. In the *Board of Trade* example the nominal rate was 20 percent, although there was a built-in risk (or lucky prospect) that by the end of the year indigo prices would go up or down. The few figures available suggest that during the period under consideration (1821–1871) interest rates did not go down. It would be difficult to argue that these high rates were the result of absolute credit scarcity. Undoubtedly, the British, French, and German merchants who granted habilitaciones had access to greater funds from their European sponsors, but so many built-in risks and transaction costs were involved that it was difficult for interest rates to decline.

The credit situation improved as the political situation stabilized, and this improvement was fueled by the stimulus provided by the increase in exports beginning after 1855. As trade along the Pacific coast increased and the transportation network improved, more merchants visited the annual fairs ready to grant habilitaciones. Local ingenuity contributed with other ideas to find sources of loanable funds. In Guatemala, for example, the Alta Verapaz authorities used Indian community funds to provide credit to start coffee plantations. The use of mortgages increased in El Salvador, particularly for activities with little risk, such as the payment of the bond required by the government to administer the liquor monopoly. Mortgages and habilitaciones could be combined as in the following example:

> The indigo grower sells the product in advance (at the beginning of the year) at four or six reales per pound, to be delivered before the fair, guaranteed by a mortgage on the finca. However, if as a result of one of the thousand-and-one eventualities that may occur, the borrower is not able to fulfill his commitment, in whole or in part, he has the obligation to pay for the dye at the price at which the lender sold, which is the same as accepting a minimum of 30%.[13]

All these credit operations made sense as long as confidence existed that at the end of the period a product would be there to sell. A great contrast existed between this period and the period of the federation when, even in the cases where the harvest had been successful, products were lost on the road to the fair to thieves or would-be caudillos (a distinction that was not always clear).

Not surprisingly, the most stable country, Costa Rica, was the first to develop a credit system. As early as 1824, credit practices were conducted that later would allow for the initial investment in coffee cultivation. In the early years of independent life, public entities such as municipalities and hospitals, together with a few private individuals, were in the business of lending money. The amounts, however modest, allowed investment in productive endeavors that, as time passed, would allow a significant increase in economic activity. While in the other countries of Central America investment was nil or even negative, Costa Rica was laying the foundations of its future economy. Anyone familiar with the simple arithmetic of compound interest can appreciate the importance of starting early.

Although Costa Rica created a credit system, credit and monetary systems developed slowly everywhere. The colonial monetary unit (the peso, which was divided into eight reales) was retained. An attempt to establish a federal bank in 1826 did not succeed. The efforts of the federation and of each state to mint currency were utterly ineffective; most of the currency consisted of Mexican and South American coins, not to mention the product of the labors of more than one counterfeiter.

Notwithstanding the variety of coins in circulation, constant complaints were made about the scarcity of currency. Barter continued to be used, and cacao was frequently used as small change. Even the half reales were too valuable for small transactions; an account by Carl von Scherzer, a German traveler, mentions that in El Salvador potatoes and yuccas were so inexpensive that "you may buy what will supply the wants of a family for a week with a few dozen of cacao-beans, which here, as well as in Nicaragua and Costa Rica, serve as a medium of exchange for articles of small value, passing for less than the smallest coin of the country. For a Medio Real you get forty-five cacao beans."[14]

The strongest push for the establishment of commercial banking came from those involved in the special long-term financing needs of coffee cultivation. In fact, the evolution of banking is a good indicator of the growing importance of export agriculture in each country. The first banks opened in Costa Rica in 1864 (after a failed attempt in 1857), in Guatemala in 1874, in El Salvador in 1880, in Nicaragua in 1887, and in Honduras in 1889.

Transportation

After independence, the transportation routes that because of the regulations of the Spanish crown and the monopoly of the merchants led to the Guatemalan capital and then to the Golfo Dulce lost their appeal and

The Economy

were gradually abandoned. Salvadoran producers, for example, began to make more frequent use of the Pacific port of Acajutla to export their indigo. The Pacific trade gained new life, fueled by the operations of European merchants based in South American ports. Trade was tentative at first but became more rapid after the incorporation of California into the United States. Changes in trade routes altered the cost structure faced by producers; during the second half of the century freight rates declined consistently, and production for the export markets became more profitable. The product mix changed accordingly.

The redrawing of commercial routes that followed was less than straightforward. With productive areas facing the Pacific and customers on the other side of the Atlantic, the objective of Central American producers was, in the end, to take their products to the Atlantic coast. However, given the obstacle of a mountainous geography, the first stage in the search for Atlantic markets was to improve the Pacific ports and to build roads leading to them. The construction of roads and railroads to the Atlantic coast implied great expense and would not be possible until export revenues increased enough to finance more ambitious projects. Even by the end of the century the approaches to the Atlantic proved too costly; it was in their urgency to get there that regional leaders made their worst economic mistakes. (The railroad projects of the last quarter of the century left a legacy of burdensome contracts and extraordinary debts that would long weigh heavily on the weak economies of Central America.)

Ports

Port development was the first phase of the transportation changes. During the colonial period and the years that followed independence, most exports were shipped from Caribbean ports. Belize became the port of choice for vessels trading between Central America and European ports, whereas Izabal, Omoa, and Trujillo functioned mainly as transshipment stations for coasting vessels bound for Belize. Nevertheless, efforts to promote trade activity along the Pacific coast began in the early years of the federation. Three years after independence the Constitutional Assembly authorized the operation of the ports of Iztapa in Guatemala and La Libertad and La Unión in El Salvador. These ports complemented the old colonial ports of Acajutla in El Salvador, Realejo in Nicaragua, and Puntarenas in Costa Rica. Neither decrees nor generous tax breaks had an immediate effect; the use of the new ports was sporadic at best, and the

36

lack of good roads meant that their use was limited to the dry season. Indeed, given the small volume of Central American exports, few ships were willing to travel around Cape Horn to do business. Another important consideration for ship captains was that the Pacific coast of Central America was not well known, which added an element of danger to their commercial endeavors.

The postindependence Pacific trade gradually increased because of coasting vessels trading with South American ports. In 1826, the British consul reported that trade along the Pacific coast had increased and that British vessels were involved in coasting trade.[15] Nevertheless, in reality only a dozen or so ships traded in those ports, whereas Belize was visited by an average of one hundred ships a year. In the latter port business was brisk; on a regular day one could see a dozen ships crowding the harbor, whereas on the Pacific side the presence of a single one was cause for celebration. By the 1830s it was possible to detect new energy in certain Pacific ports. Puntarenas, in Costa Rica, closer to the British merchants of Callao and Valparaíso, took the lead, and by 1833 its activity was unprecedented. In the same year, Guatemalan merchants tried for the first time to trade directly with their partners in Manchester using the port of Iztapa. In 1838, most of Guatemala's commerce with Panama and Peru was carried out through Acajutla, but this activity still represented a small percentage of the overall trade.

The California gold rush stimulated more navigation than any governmental decree could achieve, and its impact was felt unambiguously in the Pacific ports. E. G. Squier, the American diplomat who in his efforts to imitate Alexander von Humboldt took careful notes of everything that he observed, wrote in Realejo: "Recently the place has derived a great impulse from the California trade; docks and warehouses have been built, depôts for coal established, and several of the American steamers now touch there regularly for supplies; the station in this respect, being favorably situated intermediately between Panama and Acapulco."[16] In 1851, *La Gaceta*, El Salvador's official newspaper, made a successful attempt at prophecy: "With events in California the southern ports have acquired an importance that can hardly be calculated. We are beginning to see, in small scale, the movement that later on will surprise us."[17] Undoubtedly, the Pacific ports deserved more attention. Two new ports were opened in Guatemala in the 1850s: San José, which replaced Iztapa, and San Luis on the coast of Suchitepéquez, a port that was destined to acquire greater importance during the next decade.

The Economy

The Pacific ports, open roadsteads endowed only with minimal facilities and the legislative decree legalizing their existence, began to adorn themselves with piers and warehouses. Twenty years after the discovery of gold in California their wooden piers were replaced with iron structures. The ports created by Constitutional Assembly decrees fifty years earlier were already justifying their existence and had expanded their field of operations. La Unión, a particularly successful example of the new Pacific trade, was an outlet for the products of the fertile valleys of San Miguel and San Vicente and supplied areas in southern Honduras, including Comayagua and Tegucigalpa.

The economic activity stimulated by the gold rush was consolidated by the opening of the Panama Railroad in 1855 and by the inauguration, a year later, of the services of the Pacific Mail Steamship Company. Both companies coordinated their operations to provide bimonthly service between the Pacific ports and Panama, transshipment to the railroad and later, at the other side of the isthmus, to ships destined for New York, Liverpool, Le Havre, and Hamburg. All services were provided with a single tariff, operated in less than half the time than via Cape Horn, and maintained a regular service. In exchange for these services the governments of Central America committed themselves to pay Pacific Mail an annual subsidy to carry mail. The initial amount of the subsidy paid by each country was eight thousand pesos per year. Moreover, the rapid growth of the Pacific trade attracted other shipping companies, so that by the 1870s about one hundred ships visited Pacific ports every year.

This rapid transformation had an extraordinary impact on Nicaragua. In the early 1850s, before the opening of the Panama Railroad and the transcontinental railroad in the United States (1869), part of the migration from the East Coast of the United States to California was accomplished by the San Juan River–Lake Nicaragua route, which was shorter than the Panama route. Cornelius Vanderbilt, the railroad tycoon, hastened to secure an exclusive concession from the Nicaraguan authorities. His initiatives resulted in the formation of the Accessory Transit Company, which operated specially designed steamers across the San Juan River and ended up transporting more than one hundred thousand people before 1860. Initially, the experience nourished Nicaragua's old dreams of connecting the Atlantic and the Pacific and becoming a commercial mecca. The travelers on this route, although often of modest means, needed services and supplies, and Nicaraguans rapidly organized to supply them. A miniboom followed. Soon thereafter, however, the economic potential of

From Traditional to Export Agriculture

Nicaragua and its strategic location turned into a nightmare when the country ended up under the temporary control of the cunning and unscrupulous filibuster, William Walker.

The greater importance of the Pacific ports, closer to productive centers, implied the decadence of the Atlantic coast, which had to wait to regain importance until railroads were built at the turn of the century. Izabal was destroyed by fire in 1868, but by then few Guatemalan and Salvadoran goods were transshipped to Belize. The port had ceased to merit attention and did not receive government help for its reconstruction. Its shipping activity was reduced to two small schooners running back and forth to Belize, which in turn was but a faint shadow of its prosperous self four decades earlier. The Atlantic ports of Honduras, Omoa (the outlet for the products of Gracias, Santa Barbara, Comayagua, and Tegucigalpa), and Trujillo, which served Yoro and Olancho, changed in character. Instead of being stations in the coasting trade, they became direct outlets for a new regional trade. Omoa enjoyed some prosperity as a center for the export of precious woods until it became a victim of its own success. When the English exporters finished the deforestation of the magnificent mahogany trees that bordered the rivers, they simply abandoned the region. For a while Trujillo became the most important port in the Gulf of Honduras; in 1858, a direct service was established to Batabanó, Cuba, to transport cattle sold to feed the growing slave population occupied in the Cuban sugar industry. San Juan del Norte in Nicaragua provided a good outlet for Nicaraguan products since the Royal Mail Steam Packet Company inaugurated its service in 1848 with stops in Saint Thomas, Santa Marta, Cartagena, and Chagres. Despite these signs of life, the Atlantic ports enjoyed only a fraction of the vitality of the Pacific ones.

The growing commercial activity of the Pacific coast determined the direction of new roads. Already in the 1840s Costa Rica had a cart road between San José and Puntarenas superior to any other in Central America. In 1851, Guatemala made a special effort to complete a cart road from Guatemala to Iztapa, and a road to San José was given next priority. In El Salvador, oxcarts loaded with indigo or coffee moved from Sonsonate to Acajutla in the west and between San Miguel and La Unión in the east. Nicaragua's transportation network was rapidly transformed by the opening of Cornelius Vanderbilt's route in 1850. Only Honduras, for reasons discussed later, did not reorient its trade toward the Pacific coast.

Following the logic of the period, after developing a road system the countries' next step was to acquire that great symbol of progress of the

The Economy

Steamer in the Gulf of Fonseca, on the Pacific coast of Honduras
(from Ballou's Pictorial *[Boston, April 9, 1859])*

Victorian era—the railroad. This effort was an extraordinarily costly dream that yielded questionable benefits. In the Central American countries, the expectations of huge benefits to be obtained from the railroads translated into a shabby reality. Lacking the capital and the technical knowledge necessary to build their own systems, they negotiated unfavorable contracts with foreigners. The results were huge debts that burdened the local economies for decades. In fact, the size of the debts increased much faster than the railroad mileage.

Costa Rica, the first country in the region to have a railroad, followed the pattern of linking ports and production centers. In the 1850s a group of British speculators built nine miles of railroad in Puntarenas. A contemporary description gives us an idea of the shortcomings of the project:

> Nothing more modest or primitive than the facilities of this railroad, no terminus or intermediate stations or special employees. A clearing opened in the jungle, two meters wide and three leagues long, two tracks placed on rough tree trunks, a few little wooden bridges with ill-fitting planks, and half a dozen cars endowed only with benches and covered with a varnished wooden roof. The needs of the service did not require an engine, because

this piece of dead-end line could not count on heavy traffic. Apart from the wood that was shipped on it, it was used only for cars with excursionists or hunters. One could kill deer without leaving the car.[18]

Nevertheless, this beginning, even in its modesty, was unsuccessful; costs were too high for the economic activity of the time. In an economy with as little diversification as Costa Rica's, the railroad would be in great demand only in the coffee harvest months.

The 1870s were full of railroad projects that produced meager returns. The hopes of a transoceanic railroad in Honduras became a short line between Puerto Cortés and San Pedro Sula. Early in the following decade Guatemala, El Salvador, and Nicaragua finished the lines that linked the main productive centers and the Pacific. The slow pace of construction increased the frustration of the authorities who, convinced that extraordinary benefits would follow, were ready to make even more extravagant concessions to the contractors. In addition, high expectations were not the only incentive to sign bad contracts; rumors of kickbacks were rampant. The Atlantic railroads of Guatemala, Honduras, and Costa Rica helped to prop up the infamous banana companies, who obtained enormous stretches of land to build their empires.

Between 1850 and 1880, moving people and products to and from Central America became easier, shipping was regular, ports had better facilities, roads had improved, and railroad building had begun. At the same time, traveling time and freight rates had been cut to a fraction of their former levels. For the exporters of Salvadoran indigo, for example, transportation costs and shipping time were cut in half, even though the Panama Railroad, conscious of its monopoly power, charged the highest rates per mile anywhere in the world and operated at full capacity. The lower transportation costs implied an increase in the profit margin of relatively bulky export products such as coffee (on the average, the volume of one dollar of coffee was approximately ten times greater than that of one dollar of indigo) and, later, bananas.

Transportation costs benefited some products more than others; the same was true for countries. Costa Rican coffee producers, closer to the Panama Railroad and to Cape Horn, had lower transportation costs than Guatemalan producers. In 1858, for example, the Pacific Mail freights were four pesos less per ton for Puntarenas than for Acajutla or San José. The difference amounted to 1 or 2 percent of coffee's selling price in England.

It may be exaggerated to speak of a revolution in transport, but during the second half of the century Central America, for the first time in its history, had a reliable and economic outlet for its products. Economic activities were redirected to take advantage of the new opportunities; the export sector became the most dynamic area of the economy. Initially, changes in transportation costs contributed to the redirection of the economy more than changes in product prices. Coffee producers experienced a price bonanza in the 1830s and 1840s, but that period was a time of instability and poor transportation, and neither Guatemala nor El Salvador could take advantage of the opportunity. In the 1850s and 1860s, when El Salvador and Guatemala began coffee production, coffee prices were depressed, but the transportation situation had improved, and a certain measure of political stability had been achieved.

Alternative Products

All the Central American countries experienced the same changes in economic incentives that favored the growth of export agriculture. However, the responses to those incentives differed from country to country. The availability of alternatives, the infrastructure, and the weight of tradition influenced the export mix of each country. The degree of export diversification in each country and the specific exports had a great impact on the economic infrastructure and the organization of state institutions. The relationship between the two had particular relevance during a period when the sphere of action of the state was defined.

During the colonial period Costa Rica was the least successful country in finding a product or products to offer to external markets that would be obvious alternatives to coffee. At the same time, it had the best conditions to take advantage of the promise of coffee: with greater political stability its investment climate was favorable, it had more experience in the Pacific trade and relatively easy access to the coast, and, by a lucky coincidence, most of its population lived on or near land ideally suited for coffee cultivation. By 1856, coffee exports represented almost 90 percent of its total exports.

In contrast, in the early years of the national period Guatemala and El Salvador had products that offered alternatives more advantageous than coffee. Indigo had many virtues: its cultivation techniques were already known, it required little investment, it had a high value per unit of volume (transportation costs weighed less heavily in the overall cost situation), and its labor demands were small relative to coffee. The availability of alternative products helps to explain a slower transition to coffee mono-culture. Although El Salvador's coffee exports started in 1855, indigo kept its advantage until the mid-1870s. In Guatemala coffee exports started slightly later, around 1859, a year when cochineal's share of total exports was about 80 percent. In a coincidence whose heavy symbolism has not escaped scores of historians, coffee's share of total exports passed cochineal's around 1871, the year of the great victory of Liberals over Conservatives. Nevertheless, this coincidence should not obscure the fact that the roots of the coffee industry were firmly grounded in the Conservative period and that its development was more responsive to economic incentives (better investment climate and freight changes) than to party labels or policies.

Honduras and Nicaragua had the most diversified economies. They did not engage in coffee monoculture because, given their specific characteristics, other alternatives were more attractive. In both countries cattle raising, mining, and other extractive industries, such as wood and sarsaparilla, were profitable and could be carried out with little labor and almost no investment. For Nicaragua the San Juan River route favored in the middle of the century by would-be Californians provided attractive business opportunities. Their export statistics contrast with those of the rest of Central America. For example, none of the products exported by Nicaragua in 1864 had more than a 30 percent share of total exports. That year four products (hides, gold bars, cotton, and wood) had a share of more than 10 percent, but none of them had a clear advantage over the others. By 1884, the diversification persisted, even though the leading products became rubber, coffee, and gold bars. The Honduran case was similar, although in the 1850s gold and silver exports were particularly important. In 1855, these exports represented almost half of the total, followed by hides, cattle, and tobacco. By 1892, the importance of gold and silver had decreased, and cattle exports were almost equally important, followed at a distance by a promising new product: bananas. The previous figures hide the fact that both countries were active in the regional trade with their cattle exports. Besides the diversification of their exports, Nicaragua and Honduras had in common the fact that some of their most important products did not fall under the category of export agriculture. Mining, rubber, and precious woods were extractive products destined to run out.

Monoculture, then, was not the uniform result of greater exchange with world markets. The variety of economic activities contributed to differentiate the evolution of the organization of the state in each country. Because what was exported and how it was produced were not neutral, it is worthwhile to explore the main characteristics of the key export products.

Indigo. The production techniques of the dye were described earlier in detail. In the context of this section three specific points should be restated: Indigo was cultivated using techniques that had remained unchanged for more than two hundred years; the investment required for its production was, by and large, short-term (indigo works did not have a complex infrastructure); and its labor demands were highly seasonal. On the whole, no phase of cultivation or processing implied economies of scale; productive units could be of any size. The result was that indigo cultivation could function smoothly within the preexisting institutional framework: seasonal labor, short-term credit such as habilitaciones, and ill-defined land tenure arrangements.

Cochineal. Cochineal was made by collecting an insect that fed on a variety of cactus (nopal) cultivated in a small area in central Guatemala around the towns of Amatitlán, Antigua, Villanueva, and Petapa. During the federation period its production acquired importance in a relatively short time, and it became the leading export of the country until the 1860s. It gained such prominence that at one time it amounted to more than all other Central American exports combined. In the middle of the century, when cochineal production was at its peak, an area estimated at 2,800 hectares was covered with nopal plants.

When pests and untimely rains did not affect it, cochineal was highly profitable. In 1846, the *Gaceta de Guatemala* said that after one year, each 1 peso invested in cochineal produced an amount that could be sold to the exporter at 3.48 pesos. Robert Dunlop, an Englishman who engaged in cochineal production in the 1840s, provided data consistent with the figures of the *Gaceta*. According to Dunlop, for every 1 peso spent the producer received a net of 2.25 pesos.[19] Nevertheless, pests and untimely rains were a fact of life. A year after the optimistic report was printed in *La Gaceta* a plague of insects destroyed most of the harvest. Indeed, both the cochineal insect and the nopal leaves could fall victim to several plagues. A particularly robust and ravenous variety of the ant, called "zompopo" by the locals, loved the flavor of the cactus, and different types of caterpillars enjoyed eating the cochineal insect. Moreover, baby cochineal insects were accident prone, had a hard time clinging to the nopal leaves, and ran the risk of falling and dying. Ill-timed rainstorms could detach even adult insects, knocking them to the ground and putting the entire crop at risk. Even within the small geographic area where cochineal was produced, profitability varied greatly from farm to farm, with the Amatitlán area by far the most profitable. Nevertheless, despite its difficulties, the new product was the source of an economic bonanza during the Mariano Gálvez regime (who, by the way, personally profited from its production).

Because cochineal production required skill, dexterity, and the coordination of elaborate operations, it was suited for small productive units employing family labor. Reproducing the insects, transferring them to muslin or palm fiber bags, placing them on cactus leaves, cultivating the soil, weeding during the rainy season, collecting the mature insects and, finally, processing them in ovens to reduce them to a dry substance that served as dye were activities that demanded intense labor. Dunlop claimed that in large productive units it was impossible to coordinate the different steps and all the laborers involved.[20] When large numbers of people were working at the same time, confusion and interference hurt productivity.

Despite its rapid development, this economic endeavor did not cause the type of social tensions that coffee would produce later. In the first place, the small size of the individual farm and the fact that the nopal was not a permanent plant meant that credit needs could be satisfied with the mechanisms established during the colonial period: habilitaciones from big producers and merchants. The use of family labor and the occasional use of wage labor (often from Ladinos), together with the geographical location of the farms, did not produce pressures for the coercive recruitment of Indian labor. Also, a good part of the cultivation was carried out in municipal lands rented for nine years, the life period of the nopal. This peculiar arrangement to acquire land, together with the highly restricted geographical area of cultivation and the fact that credit needs were short-term, accounts for the fact that cochineal did not make it necessary to transform the land tenure legislation. The "model" for the *censo enfitéutico* (lease of corporate land owned by cities or communities) used in coffee after 1850 is found in the cochineal leases in Amatitlán and Antigua, a fact often mentioned by Guatemalan authorities at the time. Although it contributed to the accumulation of capital that later facilitated the switch to coffee and stimulated the creation of middle groups in Guatemalan society, the production of cochineal did not force a rapid dismantling of colonial institutions. For a Guatemalan economy that, as a result of the competition of English merchants and the loss of the credit monopoly, was losing its role in the commercialization of indigo, cochineal meant a profitable alternative. It was a transitional product.

Coffee.   Coffee production had four problems relevant to our discus-

The Economy

sion: coffee trees did not yield their fruit before four or five years; production was economical only if strict ecological requirements were satisfied; the beans were relatively bulky and thus their transportation was difficult and expensive; and, finally, it demanded more labor than previous crops. That is, the long growth period of the coffee tree created long-term credit needs, which implied the need for clear property titles and a credit system; its strict ecological needs created a scarcity criterion for land; its labor needs created tensions between different social groups; and the transportation needs of coffee producers put pressure on the authorities to improve the infrastructure.

The poor credit system and the long gestation period of the coffee plantations necessitated the creation of a banking system. The link between coffee production and banking can be seen in the correlation between the growth of coffee exports and the foundation of banks. A similar correlation is found in the creation of land registries. They helped to guarantee greater land tenure security and permitted the use of mortgages for long-term credit for coffee plantations. The first registry was organized in Costa Rica (1867), the second in Guatemala (1877), and the third in El Salvador (1882); the order and the dates correspond almost exactly to the time when coffee became the dominant economic activity in each country (see Table 2).

The ability to obtain and extend credit was still a key to economic prosperity. A discussion of the exception to the rule helps to sharpen the focus. In Costa Rica the abundance of land, labor scarcity, and relative absence of traditions of coercive labor recruitment provided avenues to avoid, partially at least, the credit bottleneck. Coffee production started on a small scale and expanded through settlements in the Central Valley, an area ecologically ideal for coffee cultivation and, given the small size of the population, abundant in land. (Costa Rica started independent life with a population of about 60,000 persons, who occupied about 5 percent of the territory of the country.) The main roadblock for the future coffee planter was long-term financing. Migrant peasants solved the problem in part by a mechanism that closely follows the theoretical formulation of investment: abstention of present consumption to increase future income. Recent research by Mario Samper on peasant farmer settlers in the Central Valley shows how they cultivated a variety of products, including coffee.[21] The peasant farmer and his family devoted part of their time to the care of a few coffee trees (time that could have been devoted to growing more food), knowing that the results of their labors would not be seen for years.

46

From Traditional to Export Agriculture

Table 2. Coffee Exports for Selected Years (in pesos)

Year/action	Costa Rica	Guatemala	El Salvador
ca. 1856			
Land privatized in Costa Rica	**751,140**	0	0
1864			
First bank in Costa Rica	**1,576,246**	192,762	80,605
1867			
Land registry in Costa Rica	**2,155,000**	415,878	275,220
1874			
First bank in Guatemala	4,464,000	**3,554,826**	1,342,952
1877			
Land registry and privatization in Guatemala	4,859,155	**4,365,585**	1,686,444
1880			
First bank in El Salvador	3,436,085	4,636,192	**1,723,465**
1882			
Land registry and privatization in El Salvador	3,512,445	3,759,252	**2,700,804**

Sources: For data on Costa Rica, see various consul reports in United Kingdom, Parliament, Cmnd. 3054 (1862), 238; Cmnd. 3582 (1866), 810; Cmnd. 4110 (1868–1869), 518; Cmnd. 1284 (1875), 1145; Cmnd. 2285 (1878–1879), 285; Cmnd. 3007 (1881), 1135; and Cmnd. 3631 (1883), 722. For data on Guatemala, see Ralph Lee Woodward, *Privilegio de clase y desarrollo económico: Guatemala 1793–1871* (San José, Costa Rica: EDUCA, 1981), 87–89; and David McCreery, *Development and the State in Reforma Guatemala, 1871–1885* (Athens, Ohio: Ohio University Center for International Studies, 1983), 43. For data on El Salvador, see Héctor Lindo-Fuentes, *Weak Foundations: The Economy of El Salvador in the Nineteenth Century* (Berkeley: University of California Press, 1990), 112.

Note: Numbers in bold indicate the country for which institutional information is provided. Banks and registries were organized after a certain threshold in the volume of production was passed.

The Economy

Little by little the area destined for coffee cultivation increased at the expense of subsistence products. This mechanism was complemented by credit from governmental institutions, habilitaciones, and exporters' advances, but this was, as we have already discussed, short-term credit.

The relative abundance of land appropriate for coffee cultivation made it difficult for any one member of the elite willing to start a large-scale plantation to recruit enough labor for the operation. Two elements, labor scarcity and the option for the potential labor to settle new land, made labor expensive and coercive recruitment impossible. Under these circumstances the ability of the elite to control credit functioned at the level of processing and marketing of coffee. Modern processing plants (the *beneficios*) required the investment of a sizable lump sum, and marketing for export demanded administrative skills and commercial contacts beyond the reach of poorly educated small producers living in rural areas.

Thus, coffee processing and exporting became the main sphere of action for the ruling elite. Here we find the social group from which emerged the future rulers of the country (Juan Rafael Mora and José María Montealegre, for example) who would define the agenda for the state. The abundance of land and the organization of coffee cultivation reduced two classic sources of conflict: land competition and labor unrest. The main tensions were found between producers and processors-exporters (who could be big producers themselves), but because the process of state formation took place at a time when the coffee industry was growing rapidly, it was not a zero-sum situation. As a result, the resolution of tension took place in an atmosphere of less conflict than in the rest of Central America.

In El Salvador and Guatemala, on the contrary, coffee production was organized on relatively large plantations, with wage labor, and under conditions that enriched only an elite—the same elite, by the way, that was writing laws and deciding the direction of new roads. Financing was not accomplished through abstention from present consumption but was achieved through complex credit arrangements that practically guaranteed that only elite members would have access to them. To finance medium-sized to large plantations, producers found it necessary to arrange ingenious credit packages with habilitaciones; mortgages of urban properties; income from other agricultural products; and commercial, professional, or political activities. Those who were successful in arranging a credit package big enough to get into the coffee business had to have, in general, a good reputation (most loans were closed with just a handshake), good

*Oxcarts transporting coffee to the port of Puntarenas, Costa Rica, 1859
(from* Harper's New Monthly Magazine, *December 1859)*

business connections, entrepreneurial ability, and good luck. The absence of any of these elements greatly limited the possibilities of success.

The land acquired for coffee cultivation was subject to litigation (part of the colonial heritage) or was in the form of government land (*baldíos*) that could be obtained using the steps established by the law. This situation also gave an edge to elite members because they had access to lawyers or had influential friends. Labor scarcity was an endemic problem made worse for the *cafetaleros* (coffee planters) by the fact that many Indians had access to land. In this regard the contrast between Costa Rica and Guatemala is enlightening. Indian communities in Guatemala had land deeds or at least claims to their traditional lands in areas not suited for coffee cultivation. This situation had two implications: (1) although they had access to land, Indian communities could not participate in the most dynamic sector of the economy, and (2) coffee planters had to bring labor from distant places. Initially, labor was recruited by offering money advances in Indian communities. Working in distant coffee plantations was not necessarily a tempting proposition for people who had the option of working on their own lands. Money advances were not an efficient recruiting mechanism; in many instances potential laborers received advances from more than one planter, knowing they could work for only one. Unsuccessful efforts were made to bring in immigrants to solve labor shortages. All attempts, from the first Guatemalan effort to bring in Belgian immigrants during the period of the federation to the Salvadoran and Costa Rican efforts to bring in Chinese labor decades later, failed. The problem of recruiting labor was a much greater obstacle for the expansion of coffee plantations than the acquisition of land. The Guatemalan solution to the labor problem illustrates the power balance in that country. When the coffee elite formed during the period under consideration was firmly established in power in 1871 with the arrival of García Granados and Barrios, they turned to legal precedents and patterns of behavior inherited from the colonial period and began to pass laws (like the 1877 Reglamento de Jornaleros) that restored forced labor.

In El Salvador, where the best lands for coffee cultivation were well populated, the advance of the coffee plantations took place gradually, often at the expense of ejidos and communal lands. The steps in this process are not yet well known, but certainly the confusion concerning boundaries and conflicting claims of lands belonging to individuals, ejidos, comunidades, and the government created gray legal areas that gave rise to conflicts and abuses. In a country where the legal system was weak and abuses of power were frequent, those having access to good lawyers and the ear of high authorities had an advantage in land conflicts. Early in the 1880s, when the process of privatization of land was already in progress, laws were passed eliminating corporate landownership and setting a timetable to finish the process. The legislation was complemented by the creation of a land registry designed to clear up confusions regarding landownership and therefore facilitating long-term investment and the widespread use of mortgage credit.

The construction of the transportation network that was needed to export coffee also imposed demands on the organization of the state; since the beginning of their independent life all the Central American countries assigned a high priority to road and port construction. The manner in which this construction was carried out illustrates how the needs of the coffee economy interacted with the colonial heritage. In Guatemala roads were built by labor recruited under a form of corvée, whereas in Costa Rica a private group, the Sociedad Económica Itineraria, supported by the main coffee producers, was organized. The Sociedad hired wage labor and levied contributions based on coffee production to finance a cart road from the Central Valley to the port of Puntarenas.

The coffee economy, with its demands of credit, land, and roads, created incentives to organize the activities of the state and defined much of its sphere of action. It seems simplistic to establish such a direct link between the economy and the state, and it is worth asking whether the state had a certain degree of autonomy. The question is valid, but although tensions existed among social groups, as coffee cultivation expanded so did the influence of the coffee planters. Those who had access to credit, information about international markets and cultivation techniques, knowledge of marketing, and deals with shipping companies were, in societies with tiny elites, the same individuals who had enough knowledge to be ministers, legislators, or presidents. The politicians who promoted road and port construction and who wrote laws were the same individuals who directly profited from coffee cultivation. Juan Rafael Mora and José María Montealegre in Costa Rica were both president of their country and its most important coffee planters; the same can be said of Justo Rufino Barrios in Guatemala and Liberal leaders in El Salvador. It is no coincidence that the turn-of-the-century politician to whom the consolidation of the Nicaraguan state is attributed, José Santos Zelaya, represented the coffee interests of his country.

Another issue that must be considered in the discussion of coffee

51

cultivation is the new economic environment it created. Greater contact with international markets created an environment of competition that had many implications. In the first place the Central American countries had no control over international prices or over the freights charged by shipping companies. Moreover, economic activities became more complex at every level. In the new economic environment it was necessary to carry out long-term investment, learn complex cultivation techniques, negotiate with skillful foreign merchants, and, above all, adapt to constantly changing international markets. This growing complexity rewarded the limited number of entrepreneurs who had the skills necessary to survive. In this sense, what we know about the handling of credit problems and about the organization of coffee plantations in El Salvador and Costa Rica, to cite only two examples, confirms the findings of studies of other regions such as the Mexican Bajío or the Cuban sugar mills: successful entrepreneurs had an acute perception of market changes and devoted their constant effort and creativity to keep pace and move forward.

In her book on the formation of a coffee plantation, Carolyn Hall describes in detail how a particularly well educated coffee planter with a knack for experimentation faced many problems when he tried to establish a midsize coffee plantation. The planter devoted "most of his reading and practical experimentation to the solution of agronomical problems," and he took "countless notes about soil chemistry, the mechanisms of plant life, the properties of different fertilizers, the benefits of drainage and the usefulness of soil cultivation."[22] This skillful coffee planter, Don Ezequiel, overcame great difficulties to keep his business afloat, even though he started it at the end of the century, when a significant amount of knowledge about production techniques had already been acquired. His problems started with the planting of seedbeds; after having bad luck planting seed, he had to turn to cuttings from coffee trees already under production. Because of rain, excessive and unexpected, and the plagues, only one-third of the young trees could be transplanted to the plantation proper. Soil preparation had its own problems. The planter expected to pay for the labor employed in clearing the land by selling the firewood extracted in the process, but his neighbors had plenty of firewood, and given the high transportation costs it was not feasible to take it to any other market. Don Ezequiel solved the problem by renting his land under a system by which tenants did not pay rent but cleared the land, cultivated corn and beans (which hydrogenated the soil), and a year later returned the land cleared and ready to receive young coffee trees. The transplanted young trees were still delicate, and more than half were lost. This fragility was a constant problem, and he had to replant periodically to keep tree density at profitable levels. The proper care of the finca, he found out, made it necessary to carry out routine cultivation, periodic pruning of coffee and shade trees, weeding, and the elimination of parasite plants such as *matapalo* (a local name given to a plant that drains the energy of the coffee tree).

The tribulations of the owner of a midsize coffee plantation seemed endless, and failure always seemed imminent. Success required a rare combination of skills that not everyone possessed. In this environment of uncertainty and endless challenges, the creative (and sometimes unscrupulous) entrepreneurs who prospered later formed the long-lasting and influential oligarchies of Central America.

The demands made by coffee on the markets for credit, labor, land, and infrastructure development can be compared with those of the cattle, sugar, mining, precious woods, and rubber economies. These products were more prevalent in those countries that experienced a slower process of state formation: Nicaragua and Honduras.

Cattle.   Honduran and Nicaraguan cattle were taken regularly to the Salvadoran and Guatemalan fairs to satisfy the demand for food and hides (to pack indigo and cover oxcarts, among other things) and as transportation (both oxen and mules were important as work animals). Cuba needed meat to feed the slaves employed in sugar production and needed oxen for its mills and carts, and thus it was an important market for Honduran cattle. Cattle, which were raised mainly in the Choluteca region, increased in importance throughout the century in Honduras; by 1855, it was the third export product (after mining and precious woods) and had a 10 percent share of exports. Four decades later, when wood exports had dwindled, it lagged behind mining but amounted to one-third of total exports. Cattle raising in Nicaragua was concentrated around the regions of Chontales, Matagalpa, and Segovia. It lost importance over time, and by the 1880s cattle had less than a 10 percent share of total exports.

Cattle thrived in the vast expanses of underpopulated land and did not create a great demand for credit. Cattle raising was an enterprise inherited from the colonial period. The cattle were destined mainly for regional consumption, and the enterprise did not experience major technological change during the nineteenth century. Because cattle were destined for the regional market and transported themselves on foot, the growth of this industry did not encourage investment in meat-packing plants with

The Economy

expensive refrigeration systems or in a transportation network. The fact that great, long-term investments were not necessary also created few pressures for the state to organize the land market or regulate property titles. Cattle raising represented an attractive alternative in Honduras and Nicaragua precisely because land was abundant and because labor and credit were particularly scarce in those countries.

Neither hacienda activities nor the marketing of cattle differed substantially from the practices that prevailed in the late colonial period. A description of a Nicaraguan cattle hacienda in 1871 illustrates this point:

> Cattle haciendas are made up of a more or less large number of *caballerías* [a unit of area equivalent to 64 manzanas, with 1 manzana equal to approximately 0.7 hectare] of land covered with natural pasture where herds proportional to the size of the property are kept. The animals are free and unconstrained by fences; their particular fondness for their place of birth is the only tie that keeps them within the limits of the hacienda. This activity requires no other cultivation or care than to burn the grass at the end of the summer to destroy the cattle ticks and other plagues, and fertilize the soil.[23]

Nonetheless, the cattle-raising business was profitable enough for the main fortunes of Honduras and Nicaragua to be based on it.

Sugar. Like cattle, sugar relied on sporadic investment, did not depend exclusively on external markets, and had significant local demand. Moreover, both industries could be carried out at different scales and technological levels. In Nicaragua sugar production expanded slowly. It certainly was not a major export product (around 3 percent in 1872), but its internal market was considerable. Sugarcane plantations supplied not only sugar mills but also rum and *aguardiente* (alcoholic beverage made from distilled sugarcane juices) producers. Production was carried out without great technical complication. A traveler noted that its growing and processing involved "small farms, each containing patches with a few acres of sugar cane, which is ground in small wooden mills driven by oxen, called by the natives trapiches; and the creaking of the wooden rollers may be heard a mile off in traveling along the road."[24]

By midcentury foreign-made sugar mills were available, but small-scale production continued to be profitable. Again, the countries had a product that was economically attractive without creating major needs for long-term investment, and therefore credit and land markets did not need to be regulated.

Gold and silver. In Honduras, in particular, mining production had

54

From Traditional to Export Agriculture

Sugar mill, 1860s (from Harper's New Monthly Magazine, *February 1860)*

been the main export item since the colonial period. Gold and silver kept their lead in the trade of that country until the second half of the nineteenth century, when metals exports fluctuated between 40 and 50 percent of total exports. In Nicaragua, the other country where mining exports were significant, gold and silver were less important, claiming a share of around 10 percent of total exports between the 1850s and the 1880s.

The technological modernization of mining implied levels of investment that were beyond the capabilities of Honduras or Nicaragua. The minimal investment to start a mine was estimated at twenty thousand pesos, an amount that was beyond the reach of the average Honduran merchant, the obvious candidate to engage in this kind of enterprise. The options available were to maintain a precarious technological level or to seek foreign investment. The option of gradual investment, possible for the coffee or cattle industries, was not feasible. As a result, Honduras had to wait until the 1880s to see substantial investments made in mining equipment, which occurred because of investments made by foreign companies.

Before its modernization, gold and silver extraction was labor intensive. Nevertheless, because Honduras was an underpopulated country with scattered settlements, its mining fields never had a large labor force. Gold panning in the rivers was carried out by women and the elderly. An American who visited the gold fields of Honduras in the 1850s described a woman "who stood knee-deep in the stream, with a wooden bowl in her hands, from which she was throwing off the earth and water, with the skill of an experienced gold washer. . . . in about an hour the *lavadera* had collected enough 'coarse gold' to equal seventy five cents of our coinage."[25] The gold collected by these people was significant. In 1853, for example, gold valued at 129,600 pesos was taken to Juticalpa. Silver extraction also operated with a minimum of technology. The simplest mills were used to process the ores; two stone wheels moved by oxen were deemed good enough. Given the location of the mines, the greatest obstacle for the importation of machinery was not the lack of investment capital but the lack of roads. The transportation of heavy machinery over mountainous terrain with only the help of mules and oxen required a titanic effort.

Mining did not contribute to the formation of a national oligarchy as coffee did in other countries. When the technological level of mining was finally upgraded, Hondurans were displaced by foreign capital because the level of investment was beyond the possibilities of the local capitalist. Thus, the specific characteristics of the main economic activity of Honduras did not result in the gradual accumulation of wealth in the hands of a local oligarchy, and the benefits of the most dynamic and modern sector of the economy fell into the hands of foreigners.

Rubber. Rubber extraction in Nicaragua is an excellent example of an economic activity that could be carried out without imposing any new demands on the organization of the state. Rubber trees were abundant in the jungles bordering the San Juan River. The organization of the business was quite simple. Export merchants acted as *habilitadores* [lenders], that is, they gave money advances to small teams of two or three *huleros*, men who went into the jungle and returned three months later with rubber ready for export. Transportation needs were satisfied by the San Juan River. The trees themselves had no owner. This system meant that no need existed to define clear property rights, establish long-term credit mechanisms, or build a transportation network. Contracts were verbal, and even if conflicts arose they were resolved without the help of state institutions. "The *habilitadores* [lenders] deceive the *habilitados* [borrowers] in the most immoral fashion," wrote Lévy in 1873, "but the habilitados, also, follow this practice and pay the habilitadores as infrequently as possible, selling their product to other buyers. Nonetheless, rubber exporters sell at 60$ per quintal, on the average, the same rubber for which they had paid the *huleros* 30$, and sometimes much less."[26] Obviously, as long as opportunities existed to make easy money in activities such as rubber extraction, the appeal of riskier and more complex businesses like coffee cultivation was less alluring. In addition, certainly the organization of rubber extraction

From Traditional to Export Agriculture

Mill used to grind silver ore in Honduras
(*from* Harper's New Monthly Magazine, *May 1856*)

imposed fewer demands on the organization of the state than coffee cultivation did.

Wood. The case of wood extraction is similar. The *cortes* (wood-cutting operations) on the Atlantic coasts of Honduras and Nicaragua had their heyday around the middle of the century. In Honduras they represented a little more than one-fifth of the exports posted in 1855, whereas in Nicaragua they amounted to about one-sixth in their best year (1849). Wood cutting, a strictly seasonal activity, was controlled by foreign concessionaires and was further isolated from the rest of the economy by its geographical location on the coast, far away from urban centers. The governments of Honduras and Nicaragua increased their income by selling concessions and left the organization of the wood-cutting industry to individuals who did not ask for further help and who frankly preferred to work without the interference of native authorities. Lévy described the operation in detail:

> Each year the place where the woodcutting will be done is decided, and workers and tools are taken there, as well as oxen and giant pairs of wheels,

which is sometimes difficult to do over the forest trails or deep rivers.

In one day the wood cutters build a small village of huts. They are divided in platoons of 20 to 50 men each, under the command of a captain. Each day he assigns the tasks to be done and the location for each worker; he also establishes the amount of the wages. Each platoon is led in its labors by a scout, a special man who long before the cutting season has gone to locate trees and mark them, and he alone knows the marks he made to lead him to them. There are very few good scouts; it is an occupation that demands energy, a keen insight to go to the shady jungle and reach without error, by climbing to the top of a tall tree, the mahogany trees that have been identified from a distance, by the color of their foliage.

As the trees are felled they are freed of their limbs and the trunks, separated from their forks, are brought to a central location to be shipped. This is a cumbersome operation: it is necessary to open roads, cut numerous trees, sometimes very hard ones, build bridges, and drag the trunks with oxen. In December, when the waters rise, the harvest of the season is taken, either on *pipantes* or on rafts, to the lower part of the river, where the trunks are piled up, to wait for the ship on which they will be loaded.

Men are paid 10 to 15$ a month plus room and board; they commit themselves for the entire season and receive their wages part in cash, part in kind. Almost all of them are Miskitos or Black Caribes.[27]

Again, the nature of wood-cutting operations did not require long-term investments or efforts to regulate land property. The organization of this activity was similar to that of safaris, and once the object of the hunter's desires was obtained, the area was abandoned. As soon as the mahogany trees of the Atlantic coast were exhausted (at least those that could be transported relatively easily), British ships stopped their visits.

Although the export economy in Nicaragua and Honduras played a role as important as in the rest of Central America, the organization of state activities was delayed because their economies had a variety of profitable alternatives and because those activities had few requirements for long-term investment or large labor forces. Coffee production, in contrast, demanded the organization of a system that could provide long-term credit, the regulation of land registries, and large labor forces. Depending on its specific characteristics (strength of colonial institutions and endowments of factors of production [capital, labor, and land], for example), each country resolved pressures differently. The influence of these first steps in the expansion of the export economy on state institutions had long-lasting social implications. The character of the relationships between different groups was determined by the weight of the colonial heritage, where the

From Traditional to Export Agriculture

Camp of woodcutters on the Atlantic Coast of Honduras
(from a traveler's account of the 1850s or 1860s)

Indian population was forced into the position of being the labor force. Where a greater Indian population and a tradition of coercion in labor recruiting existed, the growth of exports resulted in more authoritarian political systems. One of the most important roles of the state was to guarantee a labor force for coffee production. Thus, the interaction between export growth and colonial heritage had a strong impact on the formative stage of the Central American countries.

Foreign Trade

Both export figures and travelers' accounts indicate that the bases of the export economy that was to predominate in Central America during the next century were established during the period under consideration. It is important, therefore, to have an idea of the orders of magnitude of those exports and the pace of their growth.

Before this topic can be discussed further, the reliability of the data needs to be assessed. In general, the main sources are official figures quoted in newspapers or in ministerial or presidential reports. Consular reports written by European and American diplomats often quoted the same figures, and when hard data were not easily available, British consuls responded to the pressure of the Foreign Office by providing their own more or less informed estimates. How useful are the data? First, doubt exists because of the damage done to the bureaucratic apparatus by the disruption that followed independence and because of the limitations of the educational systems. Second, the political instability that prevailed most likely meant that the individuals in charge of collecting information were not always the most able or the most interested in keeping careful accounts. The sense that the collection of foreign trade statistics was less than optimal is reinforced by a reading of the comments of contemporary observers. The French geographer Pablo Lévy confirms our worst suspicions in his comments on the Nicaraguan export data for 1871: "The amounts of each product are probably inexact. We have verified this in at least two points: 1. the hides posted at 90,000 lbs., at an average of 20 lbs. each, amount to 4,500 hides, and we know in particular that one house in Granada alone has shipped, during the same period, more than 7,000 hides."[28]

No doubt exists that bookkeeping was not ideal (as a rule, errors were made on the side of undercounting, so we are dealing with low estimates). Moreover, the convention of using artificial prices further limits the validity of the figures. The *tarifas de aforos* were lists of official prices used to assign values to export and import products to calculate taxes. Lévy referred to this system when he wrote: "Another source of error is that the prices used to value the merchandise are too low. . . . besides, there are enormous and even ridiculous differences between the values accepted by each administration."[29] On the one hand, because it kept prices constant, the tarifa de aforos eliminated the effect of inflation in the time series; on the other hand, occasional (and arbitrary) changes in the price list make it difficult to adjust. Some information indicates that Nicaragua, the case discussed by Lévy, was the country with the worst statistics, but undoubtedly one has to be careful not to read too much into the official foreign trade figures. Nevertheless, the figures should not be entirely discounted. Travelers' accounts and qualitative descriptions of the economy written by local civil servants and foreign consuls tell the same story as the statistics. When a traveler writes about a poor year, official figures reflect the same; when prices go up, and an observer talks about hundreds of oxcarts loaded with coffee lifting clouds of dust down the road to the port, statistics reinforce the point. These coincidences (rather, correspondences) suggest that the imperfect figures available to us are useful to indicate general trends and orders of magnitude.

From Traditional to Export Agriculture

Another aspect of the problem that must be considered when discussing the economy is that of monetary units. During this period all the countries of Central America used the same unit, the peso, which was more or less equivalent to an American dollar. Coins from the different countries of Central America and even of South America and Europe were in circulation. All these currencies coexisted, and the uniformity of the value of the peso throughout the region can be inferred by the fact that exchange was pervasive. No time series of the exchange rate between the peso and the British pound exists. Available data indicate that during the period 1825–1870 the pound fluctuated between 4.5 and 5.7 pesos, generally staying around 5 pesos; that is, fluctuations were moderate for a long time span. Great Britain's industrial price index can give us an idea of the changes in the purchasing power of exports valued in pesos. Between 1821 and 1870, the index fluctuated between 95 and 121; again, the variation was less than 50 percent.

After having recommended caution in the use of the data, we can move to discuss what can be learned from them. The different countries of Central America responded in unique ways to the stimulus provided by the external sector; that trend seems clear. According to official figures, by 1855 Costa Rica exported 0.77 million pesos' worth of products, almost the same as El Salvador, although the latter country had four times as many people. Guatemala, whose population was eight times greater then Costa Rica's, exported 1.1 million pesos' worth of products. Fifteen years later Salvadoran exports had increased 4 times, Costa Rica's 3.6 times, and Guatemala's 2.3 times. Honduras and Nicaragua were behind in terms of total exports. In 1854, the former had a good year and exported around 0.8 million pesos' worth of products, but growth was slow and uneven. By 1892, it had not yet reached the two million pesos benchmark. The limited information available for Nicaragua indicates that its exports reached the first million pesos' worth of products in the 1860s and remained stable for a decade.

Differences in population were a factor. Per capita figures are better indicators of the importance of exports in each country's economy. Table 3 compares per capita exports and shows that not all countries had taken advantage of export opportunities to the same degree. By 1892, Costa Rican per capita exports were approximately five times greater than in El Salvador, six times greater than in Honduras, and more than ten times greater than in Guatemala and Nicaragua.

Honduran and Guatemalan rankings in the table seem to contradict preconceived notions. By midcentury, Guatemala, site of the old Captaincy

61

The Economy

General and the largest city in Central America, was, from the point of view of per capita exports, significantly behind Honduras. Even if a temptation exists to discard this observation and blame the difference on the imperfection of the data, two important elements must be considered: (1) in Guatemala most of the Indian population simply did not participate in export production, and (2) Honduran exports were mainly extractive activities (gold, silver, and wood amounted to two-thirds of 1855 exports) that by midcentury were experiencing a boom but could not grow rapidly because of the limited endowment; in addition, their profits did not contribute to consolidating state institutions. Most of the benefits of wood exports seem to have remained in the hands of British concessionaires. The incorporation of Honduras into the world market was not necessarily slower than that of the other countries of Central America. What made it different was that its long-term impact on capital accumulation and on the organization of the state was much more limited.

Export growth took place at the same time that the changes in the export mix closely followed the dynamic imposed by international markets.

Table 3. Per Capita Exports (in pesos)

Country	Year		
	1855	1870	1892
Costa Rica	7.11	20.04	37.47
El Salvador	1.94	6.45	7.57
Honduras	2.47	N.A.	6.21
Guatemala	1.22	2.37	3.80
Nicaragua	N.A.	N.A.	3.25

Sources: For data on Costa Rica, see various consul reports in United Kingdom, Parliament, Cmnd. 2201 (1857), 20; Cmnd. 737 (1873), 59; and Cmnd. 6855-106 (1893–1894), 7. Also see Héctor Lindo-Fuentes, *Weak Foundations: The Economy of El Salvador in the Nineteenth Century* (Berkeley: University of California Press, 1990), 113; José Francisco Guevara Escudero, "Nineteenth Century Honduras" (Ph.D. diss., New York University, 1983), 305, 398; and Ralph Lee Woodward, Jr., *Privilegio de clase y desarrollo económico* (San José, Costa Rica: EDUCA, 1981), 87–89.

Note: N.A., data not available.

Export Agriculture and Trade

Cotton prices, for instance, increased during the American Civil War, and producers in Guatemala, El Salvador, and Nicaragua were encouraged by British merchants to take advantage of the situation. Also, producers in El Salvador and Guatemala were interested in coffee cultivation but kept producing indigo and cochineal as long as they found it profitable.

Without ignoring the limitations of the data, it can be asserted that global figures leave no doubt with respect to the reorientation of the economies of Central America toward export production. This change can be observed in both global and per capita figures. During the second half of the century the export economy became a more important factor in the daily life of Central Americans. In Costa Rica and, to a lesser degree, in El Salvador, a rapid increase in exports occurred, particularly after 1855. Although it is commonplace to assert that the Liberal reforms of the 1870s gave impetus to export production, the previous discussion shows that the process started in the middle of the century and even earlier; by 1870, it was well on its way.

Export Agriculture and Trade

The rapid increase in exports was coupled, as could be expected, by an increase in imports. In 1825, John Hale observed that in Costa Rica foreign products were an object of wonder and that even the humble wheelbarrow was an unknown technical advance.[30] Hale may have exaggerated, but his observations explain why, since the early years of the national period, Central Americans had shown a desire for European products even though they did not yet have the means to pay for them. The liberalization of trade that began after independence triggered a hunger for imports that, because it was not matched by an increase in exports, depleted scarce currency reserves.

Initially, after independence the underground Atlantic contraband trade of the colonial period rose to the surface and thrived. Producers from different parts of the region arrived in Belize with mules loaded with indigo, cochineal, or silver to be exchanged for imported goods. In this fashion they were able to bypass the Guatemalan merchants who for a long time had monopolized foreign trade. The merchants of Belize had so much confidence in this system that they seldom bothered to open branches in the main cities of Central America; it was enough for them to wait for customers to arrive.

63

The Economy

Textile manufactures of every kind—quilting, damask, rugs, bandanas, balbriggan, cord, calico, bogotana, percale with or without fringes, linen, and countless other products now forgotten—were the most desired imports. The 1849 tarifa de aforos of El Salvador described 452 different types of textile manufactures. Among other imports were metal tools (machetes, knives, and scissors, for example); household goods, such as china and porcelain; and miscellany, including chemical products, soap, and books. Up until the end of the century textiles amounted to almost half of all imports.

Imports and Trade Fairs

The distribution of imported goods to the population at large provided the links among export agriculture, trade, and credit. Following long-established traditions, the habilitaciones arranged in annual fairs consisted of consignment merchandise (much of it imports) advanced to secure next year's crop. As happened in colonial fairs, the roles of importer, exporter, lender, and distributor were as interchangeable as those of producer, merchant, politician, and professional. The small size of the economy worked against the division of labor. Successful entrepreneurs were those who knew how to combine different activities. Discussions of the Central American economy in the nineteenth century often focus on the impact of the export economy and take for granted that imported goods and food production were somehow distributed. This emphasis on export agriculture is due in part to the availability of information and in part to the fact that it was the most dynamic sector of the economy. Undoubtedly, without a change in production techniques, the traditional agriculture of foodstuffs could grow only at the same pace as the population (and sometimes slower), and internal markets were sluggish. Nevertheless, these facts do not mean that the slower growing sector was insignificant or that internal markets were disconnected from export activities. In fact, in the colonial period export agriculture had always been strongly linked to internal markets, and in its initial stages it had to rely on preexisting institutions and had its roots in a society still geared to a relatively closed economy. Mentions of "coffee planters" or "indigo growers" generally referred to individuals who, to keep their economic standing, devoted a good portion of their time to other undertakings.

We need to restore a balance in the attention that historians devote to the

64

economic activities of this period. Commercial activity, in particular, deserves more interest. The commercial spirit was considerable, and it was universally clear that success in commercial agriculture often depended on the success in other undertakings, such as commerce. Commerce was the area where credit sources could be found, that is, contacts with agents of foreign trading houses with access to an abundance of loanable funds. Participation in commerce was a survival strategy in the ever-precarious equilibrium of the economy. The link between trade and export agriculture was clear to people at the time and could be found at every level: Indian towns from which labor was recruited also produced crafts and produce for local markets; politicians changed clothes and performed as store clerks; physicians owned plantations and engaged in money lending.

Commercial activities knew no social barriers; in El Salvador the British consul's wife observed that everyone from the family of the president on down engaged in commerce.[31] Anthony Trollope observed in Costa Rica that no aristocracy above shopkeepers existed.[32] In Nicaragua, according to the diplomat E. G. Squier, even in the best houses one room was used as a store (as a rule the room that opened to the street corner).[33] Even the legendary General Francisco Zelaya, the richest hacienda owner in the Honduran region of Olancho, spent a great deal of his time buying and selling. Every year the general took his mules to Omoa or Trujillo and returned with merchandise that he sold at a Sunday fair he improvised in his backyard.[34]

Internal trade was carried out in a network of fairs with different areas of influence. The great annual fairs, the sites for important business deals, attracted merchants from all over Central America and brought ships loaded with European goods. At the fairs, countless small credit and commercial transactions were conducted alongside major deals. The fairs of Chalatenango, San Vicente, and San Miguel in El Salvador and the fairs of Esquipulas in Guatemala took place between October and February, when the indigo crop was ready for sale, and they attracted business from Honduras and Nicaragua. Fortunately, the indigo harvest took place during the dry season when land transportation was relatively easy.

The economic year started with the fairs of El Salvador, the country where the bulk of the indigo crop was processed in October and November. French sea captains knew that if their ships left Le Havre around August 15 they would be on time to unload their merchandise in Omoa or Trujillo in October and arrive at the Chalatenango fair during the second half of the month. They went on the road again when the fair was over,

The Economy

Market stalls in San Salvador's central square in the early nineteenth century (from Louis Enault, L'Amérique Centrale et Méridionale [Paris 1867])

joining cattlemen from Honduras and Nicaragua who had gathered their herds weeks in advance to be on time for the San Miguel fair in eastern El Salvador. (Unloading in Omoa was justified for the French because Honduras charged half the import tax on goods destined to Salvadoran fairs.) The San Miguel fair, celebrated during the holidays of the patron of the town, the Virgin of Peace, was the most important fair and became a meeting place for thousands of people from all over Central America. European ships loaded with assorted merchandise traveled around Cape Horn, and others departed from Chile or Peru destined for the port of La Unión, a few miles from San Miguel, and later returned to their ports of origin loaded with indigo bales. For the indigo producers the fair was the occasion to arrange the habilitaciones that allowed them to remain in business and that ensured merchants that the next year they could count on an adequate supply of the dye. In January the fair cycle continued in

Guatemala with the festivities of the Señor de Esquipulas (our Lord of Esquipulas; the fair was named for what was considered to be a miraculous image of Jesus Christ in the town), whose temple presided over the town bearing his name. During the nine days of the fair the goods traded included British imports entering via Izabal or Belize, Honduran cattle that had crossed the border on foot, and small crafts from different points of Guatemala and El Salvador. Thus, the cycle of exchange of imports, exports, credit, and local manufactures that was to supply the region for the rest of the year continued.

Although Central American markets had been fragmented after independence, the fair network also permitted interregional trade. In 1834, Frederick Chatfield, the ubiquitous British consul, reported to his government that the trade among Central American states included products such as wool, cotton, hides, ceramics, coffee, tobacco, sugar, hardware, cattle, and raw cotton. This kind of trade continued throughout the century; in the fairs one could find straw hats made by Salvadoran Indians from Tenancingo, multicolored shawls from Guatemala, decorated gourds (*jícaras*) for drinking chocolate, straw mats and hats, bridles, firecrackers, and pottery, for example. Salvadoran tobacco was traded in Costa Rica, and El Salvador exported cotton shawls and hammocks. Honduran Indians who lived along the road to San Miguel worked all year producing candy and soap to sell at the fair. Costa Ricans harvested mollusks in the Gulf of Nicoya to extract dye and produce a purple yarn that was in much demand by Guatemalan weavers. In addition to the local manufactures, a petty trade in a variety of lesser imports existed: jackets with shiny buttons, switchblades, shaving tools, selected books on religion and medicine, and manuals for the cultivation of indigo and nopal. Also, buying and selling were not the only activities. The fair site was brought to life by musicians and soldiers, con men and prostitutes. When professional entertainment was lacking, street fights were a welcome substitute. The towns that hosted the great annual fairs cashed in on their reputation by holding smaller fairs at other times of the year. San Miguel held two more fairs in February and May, and Esquipulas organized one in March or April.

Annual fairs were complemented by smaller fairs that were regional in character and that often specialized in a few select products. Rabinal's fair in Guatemala specialized in produce; Masatenango's in cattle and cacao; Sololá's in fruit and vegetables; Quetzaltenango's and Chimaltenango's in wool products; and Jocotenango's in horses and mules. Fairs such as those of Apastepeque, Sensuntepeque, or Suchitoto in El Salvador were more local, although the latter attracted traders from a few Honduran towns close to the border. When the fairs were in their apogee, any town with some pretension held an annual one; in 1857, the French consul counted nineteen in San Salvador alone.

Less specialized and more modest were the weekly fairs that aimed to satisfy the needs of small urban settlements and their environs. Peasants came to town to offer fruits and flowers and, in turn, bought machetes and textiles. Wilhelm Marr, a German traveler who had once tried his luck as a merchant in Puntarenas, left a brief description of the weekly fair in San José, Costa Rica, around midcentury:

> The whole city comes to life as the entire plateau convenes that day in the plaza. Saturday is market day and housewives buy vegetables for the week. The great plaza is peppered with canvas stands where small merchants also offer for sale the products of foreign industry. Young peasants in their picturesque dresses squat on the ground offering eggs, fruit, butter and the like. Indians come to the market bringing maize and cacao. Peddlers, nine or ten year old youngsters, move around with their small wares, which often consist of a few articles such as needles, thread, and ribbons. Business in cheap products is carried out on foot or from horses. The placid and indolent population seems to have been transformed because they have the nature of the merchant. In market day the President of the Republic does not disdain to cut a few yards of cotton for a peasant; the Treasury Minister loses his voice in his efforts to convince a buyer that he loses in the sale of a miserable glass.[35]

A similar scene (with the probable absence of the president and his ministers) was repeated every Thursday in Cartago.

The last level in the commercial network involved the peddlers. Besides their participation in the weekly fairs, peddlers visited distant communities where they sold small imported and local items (*menudencias* and *quincallería* [trifles and trinkets]). In Costa Rica these people were called *quebrantahuesos* (broken bones), presumably because of the feeling they had after riding over the rough trails leading to the more isolated communities. In Honduras, in particular, given the scarcity of urban concentrations, peddlers played an important role in the distribution of products. Selling their wares, hundreds of peddlers were frequent visitors to the small mountain communities.

The system of fairs lost importance as internal markets expanded and as a certain division of labor permitted the establishment of permanent shops. Import-export houses replaced the great annual fairs, and a greater number of foreign merchants settled in Central America, particularly in port towns. In Costa Rica the export trade was by and large in the hands of foreigners, whereas distribution to the interior was the specialty of Costa Ricans. In Honduras foreign merchants settled in Trujillo and Omoa on the Atlantic coast and in Amapala on the Pacific; merchants in Tegucigalpa depended on credit and supplies from Belize. Stores of different sizes eventually appeared in all towns and cities. In 1858, Sonsonate had three general stores, four chemists, eighteen small shops (*pulperías*), and three silversmith shops. These stores were an outlet for the simple manufactures of neighboring communities. They displayed leather chairs, palm basketry, and screens made by the peasants of Ataco in their free time.

The introduction of regular shipping services and the improvement of roads also contributed to eroding the importance of the annual fairs. It was no longer necessary to wait for the arrival of sailing vessels that, loaded with merchandise, rounded Cape Horn once a year. Every other week the steamships of the Pacific Mail, together with numerous sailing vessels that frequented the area, could bring fresh products, thus saving the financial and warehouse costs imposed by an old-fashioned system under which major transactions were carried out only once a year. Fairs became more frequent and less impressive. By the 1870s, for example, the San Vicente fair in El Salvador was held every quarter.

Tax Collection

The rapid expansion of exports required changes in the infrastructure— roads, piers, and warehouses—and provided the funds to carry out improvements. Foreign trade and government revenue increased at the same time, and it was not by chance. Nonetheless, the link between exports and fiscal revenues was not direct. Levying taxes implied a level of organization and a capacity for coercion often beyond the powers of the new states.

In the years of the federation, fiscal problems were a source of constant friction between states and federal authorities. In the enthusiasm of the early years of independent life, taxes were abolished to stimulate the economy, without taking into account the need to finance growing administrative expenses. In the first attempt to organize the treasury, the federation was to receive the revenue of the *alcabala marítima* (import-export duties, generally between 4 percent and 10 percent, but with numerous exceptions) and the income of the tobacco monopoly and mail services. However, alcabala revenues declined as a result of increasing contraband trade, states did not display any enthusiasm to share the income of the tobacco monopoly, and the mail service yielded only small amounts of income. When Manuel José Arce became president of the federation in 1825, he found a total of six hundred pesos in the federation's coffers. A loan negotiated that year with the British banking house of Barclay, Herring and Richardson was depleted by war expenses and left a debt that later, when the federation broke up, had to be distributed among the different states. Because the states did not share the income of the tobacco monopoly a new lump-sum contribution was assigned to each state in 1827. Nevertheless, without political will the system could not work. In 1832 and 1833, all the states withheld their contributions to the financing of the federal government. Low alcabala rates were eventually raised. They did not bring in enough revenue, imports hurt local textile production, and the increased rates did not solve the income problems of the federation. Individual states were not much more successful in their efforts to levy taxes. Legislation passed in Guatemala and El Salvador in the 1830s to tax individuals provoked violent uprisings. Because government revenues were so low, wars were financed with forced loans that left a trail of IOUs. The period of the federation, in sum, left a legacy of fiscal disorder.

Little improvement in the fiscal situation took place after the breakup of the federation. Because it was difficult to impose direct taxes or to organize the collection of taxes on transactions, the best option was to operate the old tobacco and liquor monopolies and to try to squeeze something out of minor taxes, such as those on stamped paper for legal transactions and those on cattle slaughter and gunpowder. Although they were raised, the contribution of the import-export duties to each country's coffers was not fully felt until the second half of the century.

The ability to raise taxes says a great deal about the consolidation of the state. A comparison between fiscal revenues (Table 4) and per capita exports (Table 3) illustrates the link between export growth and the consolidation of the state. It is clear that fiscal revenues grew faster than exports in all countries except Costa Rica, which, having started coffee exports earlier, had a higher point of departure by Central American standards. The comparison shows that in this period the ability of the state to impose its authority in fiscal matters increased. Although some of the increase in revenue can be attributed to changes in price levels, the

70

Table 4. Fiscal Revenue 1855–1892 (in pesos)

	1855		1892	
Country	Total	Per capita	Total	Per capita
Costa Rica	506,920	4.7	5,808,474	23.9
El Salvador	446,824	1.1	6,896,000	9.8
Honduras	286,895	1.3	2,416,620	7.3
Guatemala	699,543	0.8	12,099,220	8.5
Nicaragua*	296,374	1.2	2,847,729	7.9

Sources: Various consul reports in United Kingdom, Parliament, Cmnd. 6855-106 (1893–1894), 5 [Costa Rica]; Cmnd. 6855-201 (1893–1894), 43 [Honduras]; Cmnd. 2131 (1856), 148 [Guatemala]; and Cmnd. 6855-132 (1893–1894), 3 [Guatemala]. Also see Francisco Solano Astaburuaga, "Costa Rica," in *Costa Rica en el siglo XIX,* ed. Ricardo Fernández Guardia (San José, Costa Rica: EDUCA, 1970), 314; *Gaceta del Salvador,* May 27, 1857; Héctor Lindo-Fuentes, *Weak Foundations: The Economy of El Salvador in the Nineteenth Century* (Berkeley: University of California Press, 1990), 175; José Francisco Guevara Escudero, "Nineteenth Century Honduras" (Ph.D. diss., New York University, 1983), 284; Alberto Lanuza et al. *Economía y sociedad en la construcción del Estado en Nicaragua* (San José, Costa Rica: ICAP, 1983), 102; and Bureau of American Republics, *Nicaragua* (Washington, D.C.: U.S. Government Printing Office, 1892), 68.

*Data from 1852 and 1891, respectively.

differences between countries are illustrative, in particular the difference between Costa Rica and the rest of the countries. As far back as the middle of the century it is clear that Costa Rica was in a different category from the rest of Central America. El Salvador and Guatemala, which had yet to begin coffee exports in 1855, were closer to Nicaragua and Honduras than to Costa Rica in terms of the ability to raise taxes. By 1892 Costa Rica had kept its lead, but the other coffee-producing countries (which now included Nicaragua) had increased their taxation capacity.

By midcentury, about half of the government revenue in each country came from the tobacco and liquor monopolies. These monopolies were easy to administer; once a year the authorities auctioned the right to administer the monopolies (called *estancos*), and the winners of the concessions left a security deposit or guaranteed the transaction with a mortgage on their property. The revenues from the monopolies were complemented by custom duties, internal transaction taxes, sales of

71

government lands, and smaller items, such as stamped paper and the right to organize cock fights. Later the second item in importance, import-export duties, became the main revenue producer. Its administration was not much more difficult than that of the monopolies, and as soon as foreign trade began to expand, governments began to pay more attention to it, and its percentage of total revenues increased steadily. Nevertheless, in the 1880s monies from government monopolies were still a substantial part of fiscal revenues. Customs duties were by and large limited to imports; it was easier to decree import duties that, in the final analysis, were paid by consumers. Exports were a different matter. The main coffee exporters were influential people who could organize coups d'état and who had little sympathy for bureaucrats who cut into their profits. During this period the governments of the region avoided imposing onerous burdens on the coffee barons. Undoubtedly, the tax structure was heavily regressive. No property taxes existed, and the most prosperous citizens paid the same taxes as the rest of the population.

Public expenditures, in contrast, directly favored export activities. The most important item in the budget was the support of armies that strengthened the coercive capacity of the state. The second item was public works, that is, the roads, railroads, and port facilities described earlier that had the purpose of moving agricultural products to the ports and imported manufactures to the cities. The concentration of export activities in a small number of ports facilitated the collection of taxes that, in turn, financed government activities.

Conclusion

A study of Costa Rica by itself would lead to the conclusion that the expansion of export agriculture was unstoppable and that specializing in one export product was a sure way to nourish the roots of a relatively stable and democratic state. The first part of that conclusion would be a defensible generalization, whereas the second would be untenable. Responses to the rapid expansion of the export economy were as varied as the cases considered. The previous discussion has shown that the different outcomes had as much to do with the colonial heritage as with the specific products chosen by each country to participate in the international markets.

The trend toward expansion of export agriculture seemed logical. Little effort was made to stop it, and, even if that had been the goal, no institutional apparatus was developed enough to do it. Independence from Spain implied a rejection of mercantilistic practices and forced the new states to create new legal and bureaucratic structures. The immediate result of independence was a weakening of the ability of the state to enforce economic legislation, raise taxes, or stop contraband. The federation and the new states were utterly disorganized and in no position to guide the economy one way or another, even if they had wanted to contradict their avowed free-trade ideology. Conservatives had no more capacity, and perhaps no greater willingness, to restrict any export activity that arose of its own momentum. Despite the political instability that characterized the times, the economy was not stagnant; the picture of Central America in the first decades of the century was one of dynamism in the face of obstacles and in the midst of poverty. People were ready to grasp whatever opportunity was available, be it coffee or sarsaparilla production, but opportunities seemed elusive. A marked change took place in the 1850s, particularly after the opening of the Panama Railroad, when lower transportation costs and regular shipping, together with the rapid growth of the California market, greatly increased trade along the Pacific coast. Exports became a viable option and one where wealth could be found readily. Internal production, in contrast, was stagnant in the absence of technological change. The trend favoring exports was clear, and the states not only lacked the wherewithal to influence the direction of the economies but also thought that it was to their advantage to strengthen that trend. After all, customs taxes provided most of the revenue to finance bureaucracies and public works.

Even if the key economic problem is defined as the reorientation of the Central American economies toward exports, it must be remembered that the process was gradual and took place within a framework established for economies that were, by and large, self-sufficient. The trade networks, credit mechanisms, and legal apparatus established for isolated economies constituted the initial institutional support for the new ventures. Economic sectors were not clearly differentiated. The "backward" and "progressive" sectors of the economy were two sides of the same coin. Frequently one individual had different economic personas: merchant, planter, professional, and money lender or, at the other end of the social scale, peasant, wage laborer, craftsman, and community leader. It is impossible to understand the economies of Central America without paying attention to this complex interaction between internal and external markets.

The Economy

Assessing international markets, deciding what could be produced and for whom, was a difficult task, and many false starts occurred. What seemed promising for one region was not necessarily good for another; natural endowments, geography, soil, access to ports, population density, location, labor practices, and ethnic makeup varied, and so did the economic activities that seemed viable. Production decisions in a country like Honduras, with a small and scattered population, a mountainous terrain, lush forests, and mineral deposits, were bound to be different than in Costa Rica, where the population, although small, was concentrated in fertile valleys with relatively easy access to the Pacific. As a result of these kinds of variations, Nicaragua and Honduras started out with more diversified exports than Guatemala and El Salvador, whereas Costa Rica specialized in coffee early.)

Nevertheless, no matter what product was selected, it was apparent that exports were the way of the future, and the role of the state in the economy was perceived, by and large, as a facilitator of export activities. The understanding of how to further the process mirrored each society and political system. Building roads and piers and creating an institutional infrastructure were essential steps in this process. Nevertheless, agreement on these goals did not imply that the same route would be followed to reach them. Who would build those roads? Wage laborers paid directly by planters (Costa Rica) or corvée laborers using materials paid for with the revenues of a regressive tax system (Guatemala)? The contrast between these two responses shows that not even the simplest questions had automatic answers. The appeal of exports (or of the imports that could be acquired with export income) and the price signals received from international markets were just two of many elements in the equation.

Specific institutions and customs emerged as a product of a negotiation between the traditions of the past and the promise of the future and among social groups positioning themselves in the new realities. The strength of the forces that led to the expansion of export agriculture correlated with the weakness of the states to do anything about it. Although the only option the Central American countries had was to figure out ways to benefit from the international markets rather than to oppose the expansion of exports, neither the benefits nor the costs of incorporation into world markets followed a single pattern. The balance of forces was crucial in the process of social bargaining. Iván Molina's interpretation of the exceptional case of Costa Rica makes this point: "The clue is found in the balance of social forces between merchant and farmer: as a result of the province's poverty, the commercial sector was structurally weak and lacked the power necessary to brutally subject the small producer."[36] An extrapolation of this argument to Guatemala, where the commercial sector was strongest and the small producer weakest, helps to explain the different outcomes.

Under these circumstances, choices were made as to what to produce and how to do it. Such choices had an impact on the development of state institutions because each product imposed specific demands on the emerging states. Coffee, in particular, given its long-term investment requirements, accelerated the process of state building. The regulation of landed property, the organization of a banking system, and the construction of roads became urgent tasks for the coffee producers. In contrast, traditional activities (cattle raising) or some new ones (wood or rubber exports) did not create the same sense of urgency for the organization of the state apparatus. The economic institutions created at this time and the timing of the consolidation of the state had a profound impact on the future evolution of each of the countries of Central America.

The reorientation of the economies toward export production added new elements to the social equation. A clear link exists between the expansion of export agriculture and the consolidation of a new oligarchy, particularly in the case of coffee-producing countries. Hierarchical societies were not new in Central America, but export growth changed the rules of the game. The few people who possessed the skills and resources to take advantage of the new economic opportunities also had the skills to organize the activities of the state. Dynamic entrepreneurs made the rules of the game as they played it. This new oligarchy was not necessarily a new and improved version of the old elite. Members of powerful colonial families were in a good position to take advantage of the opportunities that were opening up, but not all of them had the necessary flexibility of mind and not all succeeded. Conversely, lesser "Ladino" entrepreneurs, who under the ancien régime would have had little access to positions of power, were able to rise in the new republican environment.

Although ideology helped to determine the responses of each state to economic change, the easy dichotomous labels of "Conservatives" and "Liberals," so prevalent in the traditional historiography, do not furnish us with the categories needed to understand this process. As the preceding discussion implies, when the Liberal reforms were implemented in the

The Economy

1870s and 1880s, the trends often identified as consequence of such reforms were already clear. These trends, which led to the incorporation of Central America into the world economy, the consolidation of the state, the privatization of land, and the formation of exporting oligarchies, can be found in the changes that began in the middle of the century. At the same time, it was in this period when the differences among Central America's regions were defined in sharper contrast. No matter how one looks at this period, it is clear that it provided a blueprint for the societies that were to emerge in Central America and defined the sphere of activity of each state.

Notes

1. Héctor Pérez Brignoli, *A Brief History of Central America* (Berkeley: University of California Press, 1989), 98.

2. Victor Bulmer-Thomas, *The Political Economy of Central America since 1920* (Cambridge: Cambridge University Press, 1987), 2.

3. Stanley Stein and Barbara Stein, *The Colonial Heritage of Latin America* (New York: Oxford University Press, 1970), 137–38.

4. José María Peinado, "Apuntamientos sobre la agricultura y comercio del Reyno de Guatemala," in *Textos fundamentales de la independencia centroamericana*, ed. Carlos Meléndez (San José, Costa Rica: EDUCA, 1971), 76.

5. Troy Floyd, "The Guatemalan Merchants, the Government and the Pro-vincianos," *Hispanic American Historical Review* 41 (1961): 90. To understand the extent of the merchants' influence, see Gustavo Palma Murga, "Núcleos de poder local relaciones familiares en la ciudad de Guatemala a finales del siglo dieciocho," *Mesoamérica* 7 (December 1986).

6. Adriaan C. Van Oss, "El régimen autosuficiente de España en Centro América," *Mesoamérica* 3 (June 1982).

7. Italo López Vallecillos, *Gerardo Barrios y su tiempo*, 2 vols. (San Salvador: Ministerio de Educación, 1967), 1:45.

8. Ibid.

9. Manuel Montúfar, *Memorias para la historia de la revolución de Centro América* (Jalapa, México: Aburto y Blanco, 1832), xxxvi.

10. Alejandro Marure, *Efemérides de los hechos notables acaecidos en la República de Centro-América desde el año de 1821 hasta el de 1842* (Guatemala: Tipografía Nacional, 1895), 149–54.

11. George A. Thompson, *Narrative of an Official Visit to Guatemala from Mexico* (London: John Murray, 1829), 72. An almost exact reference is found in Thompson's original report to the Foreign Office. See Thompson to Foreign Office, December 3, 1825, folio 175, Foreign Office Series 15, vol. 1, Public Records Office, Kew Gardens, U.K.

Notes

12. United Kingdom, Parliament, "Report by Mr. Vice-Consul Foote upon the Trade of the Republic of Salvador," Cmnd. 2131 (1856), 167–68.

13. "El añilero vende anticipadamente el fruto (al principio de año) a razón de cuatro o seis reales libra, para entregarlo antes de la época de feria, entrega garantizada por la hipoteca de la finca. Mas si por una de las mil eventualidades de que se ha hecho mérito, el habilitado no puede cumplir, en el todo o en parte, su compromiso, está obligado a pagar la tinta, al precio a que vendió el habilitador, que es lo mismo que reconocer el 30% mínimum." Esteban Castro, "Estadística de la jurisdicción municipal de San Vicente escrita por el bachiller pasante Don Esteban Castro por comisión de la Municipalidad de San Vicente, 1878," in Biblioteca Nacional, *Documentos y datos históricos y estadísticos de la República de El Salvador* (San Salvador: Imprenta Nacional, 1926), 92.

14. Carl von Scherzer, *Travels in the Free States of Central America: Nicaragua, Honduras and San Salvador*, 2 vols. (London: Longman, Brown, Green, Longman & Roberts, 1857), 2:195–96.

15. O'Reilly to Foreign Office, February 22, 1826, Foreign Office Series 15, vol. 5, Public Records Office, Kew Gardens, U.K.

16. E. G. Squier, *Nicaragua: Its People, Scenery, Monuments, Resources, Condition, and Proposed Canal* (New York: Harper & Brothers, 1860), 350.

17. "Los puertos del sur han adquirido con los sucesos de California una importancia que apenas puede calcularse. En miniatura comenzamos a ver el movimiento que más tarde nos sorprenderá," *Gaceta del Salvador*, May 16, 1851.

18. Ricardo Fernández Guardia, ed., *Costa Rica en el siglo XIX* (San José, Costa Rica: EDUCA, 1970), 539.

19. The business side and production process of cochineal exploitations are explained by Robert Dunlop, *Travels in Central America* (London: Longman, Brown, Green and Longman, 1847), 123–35. Dunlop himself managed a cochineal farm.

20. Ibid.

21. Mario Samper, *Generations of Settlers: A Study of Rural Households and Markets on the Costa Rican Frontier, 1850–1935* (Boulder, Colo.: Westview Press, 1990).

22. Carolyn Hall, *Cóncavas: Formación de una hacienda cafetalera, 1889–1911* (San José, Costa Rica: Editorial de la Universidad de Costa Rica, 1978), 16.

23. Pablo Lévy, *Notas geográficas y económicas sobre la República de Nicaragua* (Paris: Librería Española de Denné Schmitz, 1873), 476, 477.

24. Dunlop, *Travels in Central America*, 100.

25. William M. Wells, "Adventures in the Gold Fields of Central America," *Harper's Monthly Magazine* 12 (December–May 1855–1856): 321.

26. Lévy, *Notas geográficas*, 480.

27. Ibid., 481, 482.

28. Ibid., 506.

29. Ibid.

30. Fernández Guardia, *Costa Rica en el siglo XIX*, 32.

31. Mrs. Henry G. Foote, *Recollections of Central America and the West Coast of Africa* (London: T. C. Newby, 1869), 60.

32. Fernández Guardia, *Costa Rica en el siglo XIX*, 178.

33. Squier, *Nicaragua*, 130.

34. José Francisco Guevara Escudero, "Nineteenth Century Honduras: A Regional Approach to the Economic History of Central America, 1839–1914" (Ph.D. diss., New York University, 1983), 345.

35. Fernández Guardia, *Costa Rica en el siglo XIX,* 178.

36. Iván Molina, *Costa Rica (1800–1850): El legado colonial y la génesis del capitalismo* (San José, Costa Rica: Editorial de la Universidad de Costa Rica, 1991), 162.

Society and Politics in Central America, 1821–1871

Lowell Gudmundson

Central American history is one of the most poorly understood of all Latin American histories, and the early years of independent life are the least well known in the region's historiographical context. Records from this period have survived unevenly because of repeated civil wars and administrative changes. Moreover, our knowledge of the period is inevitably colored by both the bitter partisan battles fought then and the sense of disappointment felt by winners and losers alike at the scant material and political progress achieved.

Despite this generally gloomy context for historical figures and for subsequent historians, many of our ideas about this period have slowly begun to change. This change has occurred not only because of recent research but also, and perhaps of more importance, because of the widespread discrediting of modern schemes of "development," of left-wing or right-wing parentage, traceable in one form or another to the Liberal project for change of the 1870s and thereafter.

Central America was indeed changed, and dramatically so, by the coffee-based revolutions of the middle to late nineteenth century but not the way that many on the Liberal side both before and after the revolutions may have imagined. The Conservative interlude was far more than a "long wait," the description of Hispanic America in this period suggested by Halperín Donghi.[1] Central American state structures were solidified in this period, even if not in the form of nationhood and nationalism hoped for by Liberals of the time. Likewise, many policies critical for ultimate Liberal success with coffee culture were begun by their Conservative enemies. Moreover, a substrata of social, demographic, and ethnic processes continued during this Conservative interlude that the Liberals could, at

79

best, influence, redirect, or reclassify but hardly comprehend, much less control.

This analysis of politics and society during the Central American Conservative interlude will attempt to suggest how the reader might rethink both the traditional scheme of Liberal versus Conservative conflict and some of the underlying social processes characteristic of this most heterogeneous of societies. No attempt will be made to recount the epic tales of battles and warriors. Avid readers can find their fill of Morazán, Carrera, Chatfield, and Walker elsewhere. Rather, our purpose will be to alternate between structural analysis and suggestive or hypothetical interpretation, appropriate for a field in which precious little research has been conducted.

The reader will be asked to suspend judgments based on received wisdom regarding this period. The meanings of terms such as Liberal and Conservative, and Ladino and mulatto, will begin to emerge as we explore the real, historical oppositions and interests that gave rise to and conferred meaning on them. Indeed, it has been the uncritical acceptance of analogies to the nineteenth-century European context, from which these terms were borrowed by partisan participants, that has plagued the more scholarly and less partisan literature as well. This situation is all the more regrettable, and inexplicable, because as early as 1768 the cleric Cortés y Larraz, in one of the classic accounts of regional society, warned the uninitiated (the king of Spain, no less), and those familiar with the conditions of the time (the locals):

All acknowledge that. . . these Kingdoms find themselves in such a deplorable state . . . that one knows not how to make them believable. . . . All hide this miserable state [of affairs], . . . what can not be hidden is revealed, . . . where things can be hidden one sees the deception . . . [and] where one can neither lie nor deceive, one pretends. . . . Knowing these facts ought to restrain me from attempting this work; but those who are knowledgeable will necessarily see that many of the things I say are true, regardless of how much they may appear fictions to the unexperienced. . . . and I often explain it with the following example, which one must imagine. . . . I imagine a city with many magicians who often entertained themselves with various transformations; at any time [of day or night] they appeared in the plazas and called forth the dead, who left their tombs and started dancing; that later the theater was transformed to reveal a bullfight, where some were gored, others trampled, and all destroyed; later a forest appeared from which wild animals emerged and thus they spent the day enjoyably with monsters, beasts, and the dead, when those who had never seen such spectres would die of fright the very first time.[2]

Our analysis of Central America before coffee, then, will include perspectives on the political standoff between Liberals and Conservatives, the beginnings of land privatization policies, the attack on Church influence and property and the clerical counteroffensive, and, finally, the economic and spatial distribution and ethnic identity of the population as these factors changed during the first half century of independent life.

The Conservative Interlude and Liberal Challenge

Usually, as Marx long ago noted, human society never sets goals for itself that it is incapable of realizing, and every new society exists embryonically in the old. However, the literature on the nineteenth-century Liberal revolutions in Central America, and especially those of the 1870s and 1880s in the north, has done little to suggest such continuity and evolution. Historians of nineteenth-century Central America have too often taken the Liberal theorists of radical change at their word, whether to praise or denounce them. Similarly, many Marxist historians have paid greater tribute in their work to the revolutionary goals espoused by radical Liberals before 1850, while denouncing their betrayal in the practice after 1870, than to the more basic principles of material causation and continuity established by their intellectual mentor.[3]

This exaggerated emphasis on early Liberal radicalism, and the seemingly cynical policies followed later from the heights of power, can readily be understood. In part at least it is the direct consequence of the impact of the writings of distinguished figures of the Liberal movements themselves, often the leading historians of the period prior to 1950 throughout Central America. However, it is a tribute to the enduring influence of Liberal ideals that the Marxist-inspired literature in the twentieth century repeats much of this view. The period between the collapse of Morazán-era Liberalism and the revolution of 1871, in particular the long-lived Carrera regime, is usually seen as little more than an obstacle-laden interlude on the way to Liberal triumph. This portrayal is given even when the author remains highly critical of the socially regressive impact of this second-generation Liberal movement. In such a view, nearly all conflict in the political arena between 1840 and 1870 forms part of a class struggle only to be resolved in the Liberal revolutions of 1871 and thereafter{ Class struggle may be seen as intraclass (progressive versus reactionary "fractions" of the dominant class) or, more rarely, interclass (an emergent petty bourgeoisie on the Liberal side versus the reactionary dominant class), depending on the particular author. The rural masses who may have supported Carrera or other midcentury Conservatives are seen as misguided in their rejection of early, radical Liberalism, mere tools used to shore up the most reactionary elements of the colonial order. }

In addition to substantially narrowing any Marxist definition of "class struggle," such a view seriously misrepresents the nature of both Conservative policy and the Liberal challenge to it. One need not embrace the recent "populist" exaltation of Carrera and the Conservatives' alleged protection of the peasantry from Liberal dispossessive policies to recognize that midcentury choices and political factions were rarely so clear-cut.[4] Indeed, the Marxist critique of later Liberal policies has always emphasized what might be termed "oligarchic" continuity. Why, then, has such great difficulty existed in recognizing the ways in which the Conservative interlude led toward rather than away from Liberal policy goals? Have historians perhaps accepted too literally the Liberals' revolutionary claims, whether to praise or condemn them?

In what follows I would suggest that the Liberal/Conservative conflict before the coffee revolution of midcentury can best be seen as an intraclass struggle among elites and would-be elites. Only in Guatemala, perhaps, can one see elements of interclass division in antagonistic bands rather than intraclass conflict among elite-dominated "city states" under one partisan flag or another. The model advanced by Safford for early independent Spanish American political divisions would seem to have particular relevance for Central America, with those near the colonial centers of privilege defending the Conservative cause and all those on the periphery of power on the Liberal side.[5]

{ In Central America such a scheme would place Guatemala City and San Salvador in antagonistic embrace, with each of the rival cities within Honduras, Nicaragua, and Costa Rica finding partisan expression for their more often petty rivalries. Within Guatemalan society the conflict may have contained serious interclass elements, but few would accept the idea that the Liberals of San Salvador represented anything other than a largely homogeneous local elite or that profound structural or class differences divided the patriarchs of the city states of Comayagua/Tegucigalpa,

Granada/León, or Cartago/San José. Although more than one partisan author, and later historians as well, saw in such bloody conflict in the provinces an opposing class structure, of feudal and bourgeois tendencies, little evidence of it, beyond grandiose rhetoric on the part of the elite participants, can be found prior to coffee's advance in each country.[6]

To be sure, interclass social conflicts outside of or in addition to the intraclass struggles of Liberals and Conservatives existed. From the Totonicapán rebellion in Guatemala as independence was being declared, to the uprising led by Anastasio Aquino in El Salvador in 1833, through Carrera and his movement of the late 1830s, to the rebellion in mountainous eastern Guatemala by the Lucíos against Carrera in 1848, to the uprising of the Remincheros there again in 1871–1873 (but this time against the Liberals), Guatemala and El Salvador were wracked by peasant-based resistance to, alternately, Liberal or Conservative elite rule. Similarly, in Nicaragua, where an undercurrent of social conflict between peasants and elites was expressed in terms of *desnudos* (the naked) versus *mechudos* (the longhairs), rebellions such as that led by Bernabé Somoza in 1848–1849, and much later in 1881 with the Guerra de las Comunidades (War of the Communities), broke out with regularity (see Table 5).

However, in all these cases the norm was for elites to fight each other viciously but to close ranks in suppressing any and all lower-class movements that threatened to overturn this predominantly intraclass or intraoligarchic political contest of Liberals versus Conservatives. In this regard, Carrera's success is the exception that proves the rule. His triumphant entry into Guatemala City was viewed with even greater horror by the same Conservatives who, after fearing a class and race war, came to collaborate with the popular caudillo. Similarly, even the admittedly popular movement of the Lucíos (1846–1851) against Carrera, this time with Liberal rather than Conservative support, was anything but a lower-class movement. This outbreak of violence was led by the Cruz brothers, Serapio and Vicente. The latter had been vice-president and resented another being chosen to succeed to the presidency, and the former was described by Tobar Cruz in the following terms: "As Tato Lapo he exercised a patriarchy over his numerous clan, from the hacienda laborers to the neighbors, as a veritable feudal Lord. Nonetheless, in politics don Serapio considered himself a Liberal in body and soul."[7]

Central American Liberalism before 1870 was as ironic as it was tragic. Although its tragedies are well known, from Morazán's execution through

Table 5. *Major Central American Leaders, 1838–1880*

Guatemala	El Salvador	Honduras	Nicaragua	Costa Rica
Mariano Gálvez 1831–1838	Timoteo Menéndez Francisco Morazán Antonio José Cañas 1839–1841	Francisco Ferrera 1833–1834 1841–1845 1847	José Núñez 1838–1841	Braulio Carrillo 1835–1842
Mariano Rivera Paz 1839–1844	Juan Lindo 1841–1842	Coronado Chávez 1845–1847	Pablo Buitrago 1841–1843 Manuel Pérez 1843–1844	Francisco Morazán 1842
Rafael Carrera 1844–1848	Juan José Guzmán 1842–1844	Juan Lindo 1847–1851	Silvestre Silva 1844–1845	José María Alfaro 1842–1844 1846–1847
Mariano Paredes 1849–1851	Francisco Malespín 1844–1845	José Trinidad Cabañas 1852–1855	José León Sandoval 1845–1847	José María Castro 1847–1849
Rafael Carrera 1851–1865	Joaquín E. Guzmán 1846	Santos Guardiola 1856–1862	José Guerrero 1847–1849	Juan Rafael Mora 1849–1859
Vicente Cerna 1865–1871	Eugenio Aguilar 1846–1848	José María Medina 1863–1871	Toribio Terán 1849	José María Montealegre 1859–1863

Miguel García Granados 1871–1873	Doroteo Vasconcelos 1848–1851	Celeo Arias 1872–1874	Norberto Ramírez 1849–1851	Jesús Jiménez 1863–1866
Justo Rufino Barrios 1873–1885	Francisco Dueñas 1851–1854	Ponciano Leiva 1873–1876	Laureano Pineda 1851–1853	José María Castro 1866–1868
	José María San Martín 1854–1856	Marco Aurelio Soto 1876–1883	Fruto Chamorro 1853–1855	Bruno Carranza 1870
	Rafael Campo 1856–1858		Patricio Rivas José María Estrada (William Walker) 1855–1857	Tomás Guardia 1871–1882
	Gerardo Barrios 1859–1863			
	Francisco Dueñas 1863–1871		Tomás Martínez 1857–1867	
	Santiago González 1871–1876		Fernando Guzmán 1867–1871	
	Rafael Zaldívar 1876–1885		Vicente Cuadra 1871–1875	
			Pedro Joaquín Chamorro 1875–1879	

the Walker fiasco, Liberalism's ironic twists are less well recognized. These ironies include the following:

1. More socially radical tendencies appeared in both Guatemala and Costa Rica despite greater Liberal military and electoral strength in the other nations/provinces of the center.

2. Egalitarian claims were made for the less favored within Hispanic or Ladino society, whereas Liberalism failed to come to grips with the "Indian question" at all.

3. Liberalism was unable to articulate a credible program for nationhood and national identity despite the identification with an independence movement justified by a cosmopolitan mixture of ideas favoring liberty of thought and action in a reformed society.

4. An occasionally scandalous tendency existed for individual leaders to switch sides, not just in coalition governments but in their own partisan affiliations.

5. The major Conservative leaders, especially after midcentury, were able to accept and benefit from many of the policies long advocated by Liberals, particularly as regards land privatization and export-promotion policies.

The strongholds of partisan Liberalism of the time—El Salvador and Nicaragua (more accurately San Salvador and León)—were able to resist Guatemalan centralism from the days of the federation forward. This ability was particularly strong during the 1840s with the Chinandega pact involving Honduras. During this time the openly interventionist position of Chatfield and the British gave Liberals ready ammunition for their positions and arguments.[8] Nevertheless, this effective home rule was only slightly less solid during the Carrera dictatorship. Rarely did Carrera directly impose or maintain hatchetmen such as Malespín (El Salvador) or Guardiola (Honduras) for long.

Nevertheless, partisan Liberalism's ability to retain elements of power in the central provinces cannot hide the fact of its limited impact. Liberalism was less obviously meaningful in those countries that were torn by civil wars, lacked an export industry in expansion, or were ruled by highly localist political oligarchies. On the contrary, Liberalism had a far clearer social significance in precisely those areas formally—one might as well say "tactically"—identified with Conservatism: Guatemala and Costa Rica. Ironically, in Guatemala Liberals clung to the remnants of the very centralism despised by their provincial brethren, whereas in Costa Rica the economic bases of Liberal success appeared first.

Conservative Interlude and Liberal Challenge

In Costa Rica, where all political factions were basically Liberal in economic terms, local leaders favored any policy that weakened central authority. Thus, even the most Liberal in political economy—Carrillo in the 1830s and Mora in the 1850s—were identified with Conservative forces regionally in hopes of defeating both effective central authority and the pretensions of neighboring Liberal forces in Nicaragua and El Salvador most highly identified with the federation project. They even sought a neoprotectorate relationship with the British at midcentury, well before the trials of the Walker crisis and its aftermath.

In Guatemala the Liberal faction was consistently hostile to old-money merchants and landowners and included a substantial number of Hispanics of more modest social origins. Here, Liberal reform of the sort advocated by the so-called *fiebres* (hotheads) or radical Liberals—most clearly reflected perhaps by the Barrundias in the federation period—could have significantly altered the distribution of wealth and power. In this regard they were perhaps unique in the region, analogous only to the so-called pure Liberals of early independent Mexico. With rare exceptions this situation was quite unlike the interoligarchic battles fought by Liberals in the center provinces.

Nevertheless, just as in the provinces, and as Safford would have predicted, the Guatemalan Liberals counted among their ranks much of the landed elite of peripheral, less politically favored areas of the province/nation itself, in particular Los Altos to the northwest. These politically "peripheral" but socially privileged elites would play key roles, first in opposing the demise of Liberalism in the early 1840s, and even more clearly later in its resurrection with García Granados and Barrios in the 1870s.[9]

Residents and political opponents of the Liberals in Los Altos were aware of the Liberals' political pretensions. The Liberal leader Cerilio Flores had literally been torn to pieces by an infuriated Indian mob in Quetzaltenango during one of the first attempts at Liberal separatism in 1826. After the Liberals staged another attempt in 1848, their Conservative opponents denounced them in the following terms:

> While the ladinos of Quetzaltenango, seduced by a few local [political] aspirants, did everything possible to constitute themselves [as a separate state], the Indians, knowing what was happening, began to rebel and protest against all the changes they intended to establish. . . . To this is added the constant influence of the enemies of Guatemala who, from San Salvador, have fomented and ceaselessly foment those seditious ideas . . . to people

who, owing to their lack of intelligence, can not even understand the danger in which they put their own existence, which would be threatened, as has happened in Yucatán, the very day the capital city's prestige and respectability, which keeps the numerous Indian towns that make up four-fifths of the population of those Departments, should be found lacking.[10]

The role played by the landed and wealthy group within Guatemala simply points out one of the great ironies of Liberalism in the region. Not only did the Liberals seek political power without radical social or economic change, just as provincial Mexican elites of the time did, but also they did so from a profoundly illiberal and implicitly racist position. The contempt felt by many midcentury Liberals for their Conservative opponents, the "serviles" as they chose to call them, was equaled only by that for their Indian serfs, the true servile group socially. Indeed, the Indians were not held in contempt so much as ignored. They simply did not exist politically in the minds of such Liberals, except as pawns in a game with other power contenders.

Nowhere is this irony better expressed than in the autobiography of one of the leading Liberal ideologues and politicians, Lorenzo Montúfar. Early in his career Montúfar was elected to the Assembly. He recounts that in a hotly contested campaign in 1848 he was joined on the Liberal ticket, surprisingly, by a priest from Sacatepéquez. Their victory was assured by yet another Liberal priest, Iturrios of Chinautla, "bringing his Indians" to vote for the Liberal ticket.[11] A convenient union in support of Liberal progress resulted: the twin pillars of the hated "servile" society—clerical authority and the illiterate Indian masses.

The pervasive, unreflective nature of Hispanic racism in this society is suggested throughout Montúfar's autobiography, and yet here was a man who never missed a chance to denounce Conservative social snobbery. He even praised, in contrast, what he interpreted as a greater social equality in the European capitals he visited. Nevertheless, he showed no sign of discomfort with the Liberal "herding" of such a fictive electorate to the ballot box. Just as revealing are Montúfar's comments on the supporters of Liberalism in his frequent sites of political refuge, San Salvador and Los Altos: sons of the "best families" won over to the Liberal cause by the strength of philosophical (and, one might add, highly abstract) arguments to which they were exposed in the same classrooms as their Conservative opponents. To Liberals such as these would fall the task of reviving a failed program after 1840, and many of them would reach only slightly different conclusions from those bitterly admitted by the defeated Liberals of Los

Altos in 1839: "If the free [Liberals] erred in making them [the Indians] equal in rights and in recognizing them as men, never was this an error based on ambition and tyranny, never the calculation of self-interest [contrary to the Conservatives]."[12] In effect, for many second-generation Liberals, the attempt to legislate equality for the Indians had all been a simple error, not to be repeated again.

Not only did Liberal ideals of nationhood and national identity flounder in the gulf separating the enfranchised Hispanic minority and the politically mute Indian masses, but also, in perhaps the greatest irony of midcentury Liberalism, Liberals were unable to consolidate these ideals even among its intended audience. Part of the Liberals' problem had to do with deep-seated localism, which economic trends after independence did little to challenge. In addition, even as an ideology of the Hispanic minority, Liberalism simply failed to reconcile its many contradictory messages.

Liberals advocated the adoption of European and even Anglo-Saxon institutions. The controversy regarding the imposition of the Livingston Codes, which led to Carrera's revolt, was only the most obvious case of this underlying conflict. Nevertheless, the most radical Liberals despised the English, at least in the person of Frederick Chatfield, and made no secret of the fact. When the Liberals did not recognize this obvious inconsistency, the results were politically disastrous. Walker, and the behavior of the United States government toward him, would cure local Liberals once and for all of any illusions regarding Anglo-Saxon intentions. In reality, English behavior toward the Guatemalan colonization schemes and the Mosquito coast claims had already made clear this Achilles' heel of early Liberalism.

Equally problematic for Liberals was the "social question." Although the claims of radical Liberalism were welcomed by Hispanic urban dwellers of modest means throughout the region and formed the basis for social movements well into the twentieth century, their meaning in the practice was limited. Guatemalan Liberalism took the lead in this regard, but even there the combination of wealthy capital city and Los Altos Liberals usually diluted whatever artisanal and "leveling" tendencies were present.

Liberal strongholds such as León and San Salvador offered even less room for a socially radical Liberalism to develop. Too few artisans and notaries and too powerful a group of Liberal oligarchs meant that the high-sounding claims of the party ideologues whetted an appetite they could not possibly satisfy, had that indeed been their intention. As the Nicaraguan historian José Coronel Urtecho put it:

> The "Leonese" and other Westerners [partisan Liberals] . . . were undoubt-
> edly more integral conservatives than the "granadinos" [partisan Conserva-
> tives]. . . . that is primarily why the sympathies of the people of the West
> have clearly been on the side of the propertied, and not just owing to clerical
> influence as Liberal historians have assumed. In León, it seems . . . there
> were not sufficient internal causes to disturb the social peace. . . . the rural
> proprietors were, thus, the leading social class in León, with their influence
> over the popular classes undisputed to that point. In none of the political
> movements was there an attempt to rally the so-called masses against the
> Leonese landowners.[13]

Liberalism's strongest intellectual claims on its followers and society in general—individual freedom of thought and action and social equality—frequently led to frustration and disenchantment. They ran up against a highly resistant social structure, one in which the hated Conservatives were not the only group who wanted power to remain concentrated in few hands. Indeed, it fell to the enemies of Liberalism, the Conservatives and the Church, to articulate a rudimentary national consciousness, most clearly visible perhaps in Guatemala under Carrera and in Costa Rica under Mora's leadership in the national campaign against Walker in Nicaragua. Rather than the "Rights of Man" and freedom of thought, this nationality would be part xenophobic, part religious, largely parochial and communal, and more inclined toward Te Deums than Freemasonry and life presidencies than contested elections. Rather than seek admission to the modern world of secular nation states, as Liberals had long advocated, the followers of Carrera shouted both "long live religion" and "death to foreigners."

Beyond the thorny questions of ideology Liberals faced other equally serious problems. Leaders switched sides with a facility explainable only on the basis of crass calculations of personal advantage. Worse yet, the Conservatives were not immune to the Liberal arguments in favor of export promotion and private ownership of land. Thus, the same Conservatives who defeated the Liberals in the 1840s, after more than a decade of severe economic difficulties, stood to benefit directly when conditions improved after midcentury. Indeed, they remained in power much longer than they might have had they been, in fact, opposed to the Liberals' most basic economic policies.

Examples of curious coalitions abound in nineteenth-century Central America. Although never as pathetic as the revolving-door partisan identification of a Santa Anna in Mexico, the federation suffered through both

a Salvadoran Liberal (Arce)/Guatemalan Conservative (Aycinena) coalition government in the 1820s and a virtually coequal pairing of Liberal regimes in Guatemala (Gálvez) and Honduras (Morazán) in the 1830s before passing out of existence. Even more dramatic were the later partisan switches of leading politicians such as Patricio Rivas and José Trinidad Muñoz in Nicaragua. Perhaps the most ironic of all was the political career of Francisco Dueñas in El Salvador. A candidate for the priesthood at 17, a lawyer at 26, the appointee of arch-Conservative Malespín and of arch-Liberal Vasconcelos, coconspirator with the anti-Carrera Liberals in 1848 and Carrera's designate and ally in 1863, supporter and ally of Gerardo Barrios in 1857 and his executioner in 1865, President Dueñas was true to only one cause: his own political survival.[14] As the principal supporter of coffee and export agriculture regardless of political labels, Dueñas dominated two decades of Salvadoran political life prior to 1870.

More general examples of the ephemeral nature of party identification can also be found. Dozens of lower-level Nicaraguan leaders scurried to join the anti-Walker side, if not always the Conservatives, after the mid-1850s. In the bastion of early Guatemalan Liberalism, Los Altos, the priest of Quetzaltenango, Fernando Dávila, was appointed by the once-exiled Conservative Archbishop Casáus y Torres to consolidate the Carrera-Conservative triumph in 1840. By 1848, Dávila had risen to the heights of Liberal influence, forming part of the triumvirate of insurrectionists who were defeated once again by his former patrons, Carrera and the Church hierarchy.[15] Unlike the Nicaraguan Liberals, and similar to Dávila in Quetzaltenango, Guatemalan Conservatives rushed to find favor—a talent they had long since perfected under the Carrera personalist dictatorship—with the Liberal regime of Barrios after 1871 so openly and successfully that a lively satirical press developed that was devoted to affixing *apodos* (nicknames) to those of recent partisan conversion within the government.[16]

The blood of common class and ethnic origin proved far thicker than the water of partisan political identification throughout the nineteenth century in Central America. "Civilization" and "progress" came first, however bloody the conflict regarding which ideal, aristocratic or bourgeois, was to guide the common prize of Creole/Ladino culture: the state. Although it would be an exaggeration to say that ideology was irrelevant, undoubtedly party identification was viewed far more as a vehicle to power than as a guide or even an a posteriori justification for policy.

Indeed, the somewhat pained judgment of the Nicaraguan historian

Society and Politics

Jerónimo Pérez regarding the notoriously bloody and petty conflicts of the federation era in his homeland could well be applied to much of the isthmus during this entire period:

> Our tendency [is] to convert into a public issue what should not go beyond the limits of the private. . . . the parties . . . proclaim no system, nor defend different principles. . . . Thus it is that party names have been no more than nicknames to distinguish one from the other. . . . neither the "serviles," the "desnudos," the "mechudos," the "timbucos," the "calandracas," the "Conservatives," nor the "Liberals" have been what these words signify. In Nicaragua, without exception, all love the Republic; unfortunately only for themselves, excluding all others.[17]

However, perhaps the most serious damage to Liberalism throughout the region by this largely utilitarian and ephemeral definition of partisanship was the voluntary identification of the area's quintessential Liberals—the coffee elite of Costa Rica—with the Conservative side. Although this identification had little relationship to local policymaking, its logic deprived Liberalism of an important and natural ally. This weakening of Liberalism only worsened the prospects of a movement already weakened by unpopular coalitions with the Conservatives and the unprincipled switching of allegiance to and from the movement by well-known caudillos.

Once in power and safe from Liberal armies and reprisals at home or abroad, Conservatives frequently pursued many of the Liberal policies that favored export growth and private initiative in agriculture. Indeed, few Conservatives fit the model painted by the Liberals of "El Indio" (the quintessential and telling "low-brow" Liberal epithet used to describe Carrera), oblivious to the demands of the modern world. Perhaps only Malespín in El Salvador (1844–1845) could be seen as a blindly anti-Liberal reactionary, and that view was more the result of his role as Carrera's designate than because of any systematic policies of his own.

The Conservatives seen more frequently were those who sought to benefit from a measure of Liberal policy success and to claim credit for it whether due or not. Carrera himself never tired of claiming credit for the growth of exports during the 1850s. His successor, Vicente Cerna, was even more well disposed toward exports and policies designed to increase them.[18] Similarly, the Nicaraguan Conservatives who ruled for thirty years following the defeat of Walker laid the groundwork for coffee and sugar export agriculture while also building railroads. Although Gerardo Barrios

92

is usually seen as the precursor of Liberal triumph in El Salvador, Conservative leaders such as Dueñas and Gallardo were more directly responsible for coffee's take-off. Even in Costa Rica, where partisan labels counted for little in general, the overthrow of the so-called Conservative Mora in 1859 came after a ten-year dictatorship of coffee export interests at the hands of his brother-in-law, Montealegre, another leading coffee exporter.

With antecedents such as these in mind, no longer can one seriously argue that coffee and Liberalism were synonymous in Central America. Coffee allowed for a second coming of Liberalism, to be sure, but proexport policies were anything but a Liberal monopoly. Indeed, if coffee revolutionized Central America, then the Liberal reforms were more capstone than cornerstone in the process. The gold rush era, described in detail in the preceding essay by Lindo-Fuentes, was more of an ally of the Liberals than their own foresight or any "obscurantism" on the part of the Conservatives. One of the most important aspects of this Conservative synthesis of Liberal policy initiatives has to do with land tenure, and this issued is addressed in detail below.

From Corn and Cattle to Coffee: Land Tenure Policies

Where we once saw the Liberal reforms of the 1870s as a draconian policy designed to privatize landownership and transform agriculture in a matter of months, it is now clear that the process was far more complex in practice. This complexity can be seen in three distinct aspects: the diversity of land tenure systems inherited from the colonial period and the repeated "false starts" of Liberal policy during the federation era; the process by which, during the 1840–1870 period, privatized production and export agriculture were furthered by Liberal and Conservative alike; and, finally, the extraordinary diversity of outcomes, both political and socioeconomic, of Liberal reform once consolidated. Although this last aspect covers an area considerably beyond the scope of this essay, we should point out that such outcomes ranged from wholesale privatization and colonization in Costa Rica, to private ownership combined with wage labor in El Salvador, to a myriad of solutions throughout Guatemala—the best known involving seasonal migration of Indian labor to the Costa Cuca of the west-southwest—to the fundamental precariousness, if not insignificance, of privatization in land tenure in much of Honduras and Nicaragua.[19] Indeed, much of the land tenure agenda of classic liberalism in Central America would be embraced only in the 1890s with Zelaya in Nicaragua and even later in Honduras. As late as the mid-twentieth century a common lands system predominated in Honduran coffee production, a juxtaposition of forms the irony of which is perhaps clear only to students of coffee culture elsewhere in the isthmus.

Although undoubtedly differences existed between the Liberals of the 1820s and 1830s and those of the 1870s, they all tended to assume that communal ownership of land was, to some degree, an obstacle to the development of market production and exports. For them, corn and cattle, the bases of most colonial agriculture, were activities adapted to an annual cropping cycle and open-range grazing and poorly suited to the need for long-term investment in and improvement of land for export crops. Coffee, the perennial crop with a three- to five-year investment requirement prior to any return, came close to being the perfect antithesis to corn and cattle. It was a crop whose technical conditions of production drove forward the privatization process advocated by the Liberals far beyond that of even the earlier export staples of indigo and cochineal.

However, the first generation of Liberals seemed to believe that private ownership of land could be fostered in addition to all those complex categories inherited from the colonial past. They clearly recognized that land itself was virtually never in short supply. Their successors, half a century later, had the fateful task of resolving the more pressing problems concerning shortages of labor and capital, along with the much debated land question. The earliest Liberal federation decrees favoring land privatization, in particular one from 1825 (number 27, 19-1-1825, section 21), specifically noted that such concessions were not to conflict with "common lands of the villages, for both planting and seasonal clearing as well as for pasture of all classes of livestock."[20]

During the controversy regarding the grants to foreign colonization schemes in the decade of the 1830s, the soon-to-be president of Guatemala, Mariano Rivera Paz, asked rhetorically of his opponents: "The contract cedes the public lands for settlement, allowing the use of the hills, forests, and rivers. What is understood by use? Just because the Company has use [rights], how does this deny the same use [rights] to all other inhabitants?"[21] The answer to just such a question would be given by events after 1850, and it would not be the one suggested by Rivera.

Clearly, such legislators presumed virtually limitless land resources would be available to perspective "owners." Nevertheless, because such property owners would be obligated to respect not only communal "seed beds or plantings" but also "seasonal clearings and all forms of pasture," perhaps no great transformation in land tenure or a rush to the countryside could be expected to claim rights as dubious as these. Indeed, foreign observers repeatedly commented on both the scarce population in much of the region and this, for them, "quaint" practice and assumption on the part of even the Liberals regarding the compatibility of colonial and fully privatized land tenure categories. Dunlop was categorical in his remarks in 1847: "Not one one-hundreth of the available soil is cultivated. . . . the value of the land is nearly nominal, and, in ordinary case, is actually of no marketable value whatever, except in the vicinity of some large town."[22] He then went on to note, however, that close-in land used for cochineal in Guatemala or coffee in Costa Rica was worth from sixty to ninety pounds sterling per acre.

In addition, although early Liberal visions were seen by some as quaint in their impracticality, their actions were often disastrously clumsy. Calls for private landownership were usually heard in unison with attacks on Church property. In this case, no amount of ridicule of obscurantism and superstition could convince villagers that they were better off deprived of herds and pastures held collectively under Church sanction. Liberals seemed to assume that, instead of being their own strategic political challenge, it was somehow the duty of the masses to separate their interests from those of the "moribund" Church hierarchy. Time after time the opposite proved to be the case.

Even more damaging identification of Liberal policy favoring private ownership of land with influence-peddling emerged as early as the 1830s. The prolonged opposition of Chiquimula to the Gálvez regime and its concessions to English and Belgian colonization schemes is but the best known of these municipal-level conflicts. The dozens of cases of land titling of village property and the awarding of monopolistic contracts to Liberal political figures represent some of the least attractive features of early, "enlightened" Liberalism in Central America. Morazán's handling of lumber concessions on the Honduran coast during the 1830s without authorization from the federation he repeatedly saved from extinction is a particularly telling example. This particular episode did little to convince the skeptics of either the Liberals' honesty or respect for central, federation authority. Indeed, as Wortman put it, Morazán's administration in Honduras showed all the signs of localistic autonomy that he attacked elsewhere in the name of unity and the federation.[23] Unfortunately, in all the republics, from Guatemala under Carrera and then Barrios to Costa Rica under Mora and then Montealegre, the common belief that Liberal policy was simply well-embellished political favoritism appeared to be confirmed by the repeated confiscation of opponents' landed property and its transfer to the victors' portfolio.

Liberal misunderstandings and policy mistakes aside, however, widely divergent situations existed in the isthmus regarding land tenure. In the cattle range areas of Honduras, Nicaragua, and Costa Rica, private ownership of land meant relatively little, with much of the peasantry using the heavily forested countryside for sporadic planting breaks in addition to the ejidos or measured planting lands of the villages. Here, land itself was rarely the key issue; rather, access to scarce capital and labor was the main concern. Moreover, with the exception of Costa Rica and its coffee economy after the 1840s, little success was experienced in export agriculture. Therefore, little was accomplished by Liberals in land tenure, and this issue was not as conflictive as it would become elsewhere.

In the more heavily populated areas of Guatemala and El Salvador, however, the land tenure situation was more complex. In the Indian highlands of Guatemala most land conflicts involved native communities fighting among themselves, and Liberals did little, beyond their anti-Church policies, to change this situation before or after 1871. In effect, as Carol Smith has argued, the Carrera regime gave rise to a unique regional economy here, which will be discussed later.[24] Its regional market town structure and popular basis for artisanal specialization and exchange were unique in the isthmus and have remained so to the present day. Similarly, Liberals went slow in attempting any radical transformation in land tenure systems in the Indian heartland of Guatemala after 1871.

However, where Indian and Ladino populations coexisted in relatively comparable numbers, as in El Salvador and areas southwest and east of Guatemala City, Liberal initiatives had a far greater impact, an impact that could have been anticipated from colonial practice, and they were continued by their Conservative opponents, perhaps unwitting allies in this area. The situation of Indian communities varied enormously in these areas. Some faced intense pressures to share their land and resources and to assimilate through race mixture. In these cases they approximated the experience of the few Indian communities of highland Costa Rica, virtually eradicated from collective memory by the coffee revolution of the 1840s. However, many others held abundant lands, some rented to Ladinos and all coveted by Liberal reformers and Ladinos alike. Here it was not so much the "lazy Indian" as the "rich Indian" made lazy by excessive wealth (land) that focused Liberal/Ladino envy and demands for change.

The solution to this problem, sanctioned since late colonial times, had been the forced rental of "unused" lands of Indian villages to Ladino outsiders. This policy gained new meaning and momentum under both Liberal and Conservative programs promoting exports. In effect, communities were obliged to give over in perpetual leases (*censo enfitéutico* or *enfiteusis*) unused lands to those who would grow coffee or other export crops. The change from an annual cropping cycle, based on shifting slash-and-burn methods, to a perennial crop with heavy permanent labor investment in a particular plot of land had profound implications that were evident to all involved. Not only did perennial cropping vastly increase the land that could be defined as "unused" (held in reserve in the old, rotational system no longer to be used), but it also did so whether sanctioned by Liberals or, as happened more often, by Conservatives such as Carrera, Cerna, or Dueñas. Although they perhaps did not assist in the development of coffee culture as much as the programs of Carrillo in Costa Rica and Gerardo Barrios in El Salvador, with their free land and seedlings programs for coffee growers, the perpetual leases, developed most fully by the Conservatives, were of critical importance in the transitions of the 1870s. Indeed, Justo Rufino Barrios most often deeded over land in coffee, including to himself, that was long held with Conservative sanction under perpetual lease. Decree number 170 of January 8, 1877, finally eliminated this form of property altogether in Guatemala, and its terms are a particularly good example of Liberal thinking on the issue:

> Whereas: the contract for censo enfiteusis is an institution out of step with the economic principles of the day, . . . although it has facilitated the distribution of real estate . . . the limitation on effective ownership . . . and the obstacles to the recognition of direct [freehold] ownership, necessarily produce an obstacle to the free exchange of property, leading to the lowering of its value and the lack of incentive for improving [the land] for the benefit of agriculture.[25]

In effect, it had only now outlived its considerable usefulness for the Liberals.

The length of this process of privatization, only culminating with the regimes of the 1870s in Guatemala and El Salvador, has been revealed most clearly in recent works by Castellanos Cambranes and Lindo-Fuentes.[26] The former shows how great a diversity of experience existed in Guatemala and how widespread the issues of "unused" lands and perpetual leases were. This situation was true not only in the traditional areas of late

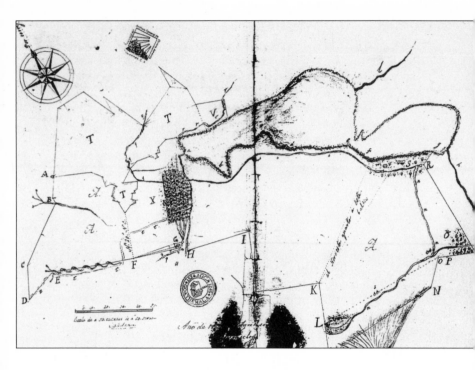

Common Lands in Guatemala, 1834. Survey for Amatitlán, southwest of Guatemala City, of its 90 caballerías (1 = 45 hectares). When measured again in 1865, the total was 171 caballerías. (Archivo General de Centroamérica, Sección Tierras—Amatitlán, paquete 1, expediente 5)

colonial rental, from Chiquimula in the east to Escuintla in the southwest, but also in the far west and southwest, where most earlier authors portrayed a process of titling of baldíos to coffee growers relying on forced Indian labor from the distant highlands. In several cases the land in question was claimed by neighboring highland communities but had been pried loose by a combination of forced rental and political intrigue.

For his part, Lindo-Fuentes sharply reduces the earlier estimates of Browning and Menjívar as to the amount of land privatized after the late 1870s in El Salvador, from between 25 and 50 percent of arable land to half this amount at most.[27] The corrosive effects of the gold rush–era trade and exports to California, along with the coffee trade itself, had led to a gradual process of decomposition of common lands under Dueñas as much as

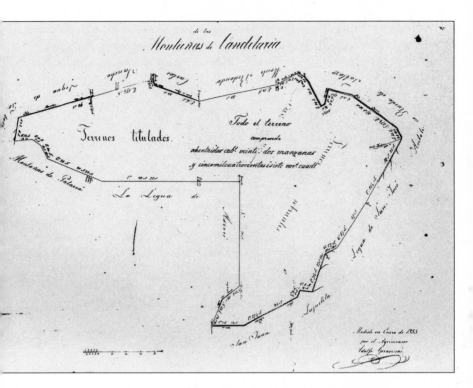

Common Lands in Costa Rica, 1853. Residents of Desamparados, south of San José, request excess lands (terrenos sobrantes on the right), long held without formal title. (Archivos Nacionales de Costa Rica, Contencioso Administrativo, "Tierras," No. 2748)

under Barrios before or under those who would follow in the 1880s. In both cases (the California trade and the beginnings of coffee cultivation), and whatever the legal framework involved, from perpetual lease to outright purchase of supposedly public land, the Conservative interlude witnessed much of the land privatization process long thought the exclusive work of Liberal revolutionaries. Although they no doubt were its intellectual authors, Liberals could only claim to have consolidated and accelerated the triumph of land privatization. Conservative opposition was not the major obstacle here. Indeed, they collaborated more or less willingly on this score after midcentury.

Liberal difficulties had little to do with Conservative opposition to land tenure policies. Rather, they had to do with the widespread animosity generated by their earlier attacks on the Church and all it represented. In claiming to oppose their sworn enemies—the Church and the Conservatives—the heaviest Liberal blows fell on the former, and the communal, village economy it legitimized and helped organize, without mortally wounding the latter. Although such an outcome is hardly surprising, given the largely common class origins of the two groups in conflict, it was through their policies on the Church that Liberals most consistently alienated the masses without routing their Conservative enemies. Indeed, the combination of Liberal Church and common lands policies that infuriated the masses, neither of which Conservatives invariably opposed, helps explain the remarkably long absence from power of the northern Liberals, particularly in Guatemala. It is to these failed attempts at the creation of a national identity based on secular, largely anticlerical ideas that we must now turn.

The Church Question: Mortmain and Life's Blood

If any one feature defined Liberalism in Central America before 1860, it was the often violent opposition to the Church and its role in society and politics. The Liberals, both first- and second-generation, opposed ecclesiastical property in mortmain not only because of its impact as a tax-exempt enterprise on an always agonizing fiscal situation but also because it blocked the free circulation and maximum growth in public wealth. Because the positivist imagery and metaphors were more widely diffused after midcentury, an identification grew between the circulation of private property in the "body politic" and their biological equivalents, that is, the blood, source, and support of life. In such an ideological scheme, property in mortmain (*manos muertas*) became not only an inefficient or elitist institution but also the source of economic and social backwardness; it was not just a mistaken policy, but evil itself.

Liberal opposition was directed both at the Church's economic power and its social and intellectual influence. Although the Church was unable to resist the Liberal challenge directly, especially with regard to its economic strength, it proved highly resourceful in exploiting lower-class religious fervor and xenophobia to counter Liberal claims for a secular national order. Moreover, many priests, particularly in the provinces, were supportive of parts of the Liberal agenda, especially when, as in El

Salvador's perennial claims to a bishopric, their own institutional interests might be served also. Overall, the social influence of the Church was not so readily uprooted as its economic base. In the process villagers lost ground at least as often as the institutional Church, and Liberals alienated both religious xenophobes and the more radical within their own ranks who rejected any marriage of convenience between Liberals and churchmen in the provinces.

In attacking all forms of Church property Liberals were only following a well-worn trail leading back to late colonial times. The Bourbon monarchs had already launched a frontal assault on the Church with the expulsion of the Jesuits and the seizure of their property in 1767 and damaged the Church more seriously with the Consolidación de Vales Reales (which can be defined loosely as the Consolidation of Royal Obligations) in 1804 and thereafter. The economic and political consequences of the latter were particularly disastrous and may have contributed to the growth of pro-independence opinion throughout the colonies.

A great deal of confusion has long surrounded the topic of Church wealth and the Liberal attack on it in Central America as elsewhere in Latin America. Part of this confusion can readily be traced to partisan, Liberal exaggerations in the heat of political battle. However, the complexity of Church wealth requires a brief commentary prior to discussing Liberal policy challenges themselves.

Generally speaking, the Church was both the society's principal (and only legal) banker and a major property holder in diverse forms. As a rule the Church's banking functions were most highly developed in export-oriented economies and regions, whereas its property holding in lay brotherhood (*cofradía*) funds predominated in the more peripheral areas. Rarely, essentially only in Guatemala, the Church held vast agricultural properties; more often its real estate was urban-based. The sugar estates of Guatemala, where five of the largest eight were held by regular orders and the largest, owned by the Dominicans, had seven hundred slave laborers, were a rare exception not to be found elsewhere in Central America or among the secular (nonorder) branches of the Church.

Further complexity existed within each branch of Church financial activity. Its banking functions were essentially of two kinds: *capellanías* (chaplaincies or chantries) and *censos* (annuities). Although in theory both were transactions with mortgage guarantees, the former were actually liens on property executed in favor of the Church to support masses or pious works, whereas the latter were loans of Church funds guaranteed by

101

property. Truly commercial lending was concentrated in the censo category, on a yearly basis, whereas the capellanías were perpetual loans or liens, often against cattle ranches whose market value might very well not correspond to the stated principal of the various capellanías weighing against it. Thus, the principal of the capellanías constituted a sum on which a yearly payment would be calculated in exchange for masses that might be sung by a family member of the property owner who had entered the priesthood.

Logically, expropriating Church wealth in censos might mobilize liquid funds, whereas similar attacks on capellanías would yield little in the short run because stated mortgage obligations had little relationship to commercial reality. Moreover, any such attack would fall more heavily on the indebted property holder than on the institutional Church itself. Thus, Liberals would eventually come to argue that all landholders, Liberal and Conservative alike, should be liberated from such medieval debt rather than seeking to auction properties for their mortgage value. Once they reached this level of sophistication in their policies, Liberals were joined by opportunistic Conservatives, more anxious to relieve themselves of their commercial rather than their moral obligation. After midcentury the behavior of leading Conservatives in this regard is perhaps the clearest confirmation of that late-twentieth-century critique of geopolitical posturing in the isthmus: where material interests begin ideologies end.

On the side of real property holdings the situation was equally complex. Although the regular orders, in particular the Dominicans in Guatemala, held working sugar, wheat, and cattle estates, relatively little of Church wealth was tied up in landownership per se. Indeed, speculative urban real estate was far more likely the basis of the Church's portfolio. However, the greatest part of the real property controlled by the Church, that of the cofradías, was actually administered by the Church in the name of specific communities and groups of laymen. In the diocese of Guatemala alone in 1800, there were 1,703 cofradías with 581,833 pesos worth of property. Although we lack complete figures for the expropriations in 1829, the San Gerónimo sugar estate was sold to foreign interests for the astronomic sum of 253,526 pesos, 4 1/4 reales, and the proceeds from the sale of all twenty-two rural properties together amounted to 378,480 pesos versus 88,065 pesos for twenty-seven urban holdings. In contrast, the seizures carried out by Gálvez between 1831 and 1837 in Guatemala produced only 181,708 pesos for the federation government.[28] It was the attack on this form of property that both offered the greatest short-term financial gain to the Liberals and generated the most conflict with villagers who saw the Liberals as thieves more than they saw the Church as their exploiter. This attack was made even worse by the frequent practice of "fire-sale" liquidations of such property to Liberal politicians and, once again, the frequent Conservative opportunist.

The major Liberal attack on Church property in Guatemala took place under Morazán's leadership in 1829. Under a decree of July 28, 1829, the regular orders, in particular the Dominicans, were expelled to Cuba along with the archbishop, and their property was seized. A total of 289 clerics were exiled at this high point of federation and Liberal anticlericalism.[29] Fitful revivals of anticlerical policy, especially in the provinces, were noted in the mid-1830s, mid-1840s, in Costa Rica in 1859, and in El Salvador under Gerardo Barrios in the early 1860s. In each case the Church was drained of much of its liquid wealth, and chaotic attempts were made to seize and auction real property.

Perhaps the greatest success of these early campaigns was the seizure of the Dominicans' vast properties by Morazán in 1829. Moreover, the Liberal campaigns of the mid-1830s served as the pretext for the permanent exemption of coffee from any tithe payment in Costa Rica. This act, just as the Dominican expropriations in Guatemala, the sales of cattle herds in Nicaragua and Costa Rica in the 1840s, and the abolition of capellanías in El Salvador in the 1860s, would not be overturned by later Conservative regimes under Carrera in Guatemala or Dueñas in El Salvador or under the various rulers of Nicaragua and Costa Rica who often claimed to be Conservatives at the same time that they abolished forms of Church property. However, the exemption from the tithe was not achieved by coffee growers in the north until the Liberal revolutions of the 1870s.

The events leading to the fall of Juan Rafael Mora from the Costa Rican presidency in 1859 shows just how close a fit existed among these economic and ecclesiastical variables.[30] Mora, along with the Argentine investor Crisanto Medina, had attempted to form a state bank while expelling the newly appointed Bishop Llorente y Lafuente for his public criticism of the regime. Mora's opponents within the coffee oligarchy deposed him partly out of fear of the lending competition that would result from such a state bank, and the Church supported the coffee oligarchy. In the coffee merchant regime of Costa Rica the bishop had little reason to think that any ecclesiastical lending predominance might be restored. However, his hopes for a reinstatement of the tithe on coffee production itself proved just as groundless.

Society and Politics

Virtually everywhere in Central America Conservatives refused to undo Liberal initiatives from which they had also benefited, especially where an expanding export trade was involved. In 1844, even Carrera, the most famous of the Conservative defenders of the Church, accepted the "gift" by a grateful republic of a sugar estate in Palencia in eastern Guatemala that had been seized from the Dominicans in 1829. His consort's allegedly vicious exploitation of food grain supplies in the area was used as a justification for participation in the Lucío rebellion of the late 1840s. Carrera returned the gift to the state in 1847, with the vain hope of thereby pacifying the situation.[31] As elsewhere in Central America, Conservatives in Guatemala could be made to see the virtues of the Liberal program of seizure of Church property under the right circumstances.

Secularization and the Clerical Counteroffensive

Secular political authority, both Liberal and Conservative, proved highly successful in divesting the Church of its worldly possessions. Nevertheless, Liberals proved far less successful in their attempts to challenge the Church ideologically. Major efforts at secularization, particularly during the 1830s, proved disastrous. Moreover, the widespread warfare and cholera epidemics of the late 1830s and mid-1850s, the trying times of Central American nationhood internally with Carrera and externally with the Walker affair, made a mockery of the Liberal promise of progress and well-being along northern European or Anglo-Saxon institutional lines.

The major attempt at secularization took place in 1837 under Morazán and Gálvez. The major components of this campaign were the developments associated with the Livingston Codes, which included the law sanctioning divorce and mandating inheritance rights for illegitimate children, lay education, and support for European Protestant immigration to develop the region economically. Although each of these initiatives could be defended as progressive and necessary, they exposed the Liberals to criticism not just from infuriated Conservatives and clerics but also from a commoner society that saw in these laws no small degree of irrelevance and hypocrisy.

The innovations during the era of the Livingston Codes (trial by jury and divorce and inheritance rights, for example) were defended as socially leveling, democratic policies by their supporters. However, in a society so badly divided ethnically, linguistically, and socially, the laws threatened judicial chaos more than reform. For example, how such a system of trial by jury was to be developed in an overwhelmingly illiterate and multilingual society, other than as a basically elitist and thinly veiled Liberal political tribunal, was lost in the largely doctrinaire debate over its approval.

In explaining the defeat of the codes and their innovations, Montúfar once again placed the blame on the masses in openly racial terms:

> The Livingston Code was no more than a pretext. In the [Carrera] Revolution one sees with total clarity the hand of the clergy, which one day takes advantage of an eclipse, another of thunder, another of an earthquake, another of a volcanic eruption, and still another of the Livingston Code to regain control over minds and establish its absolute empire as in the Middle Ages. . . . Some will say that the people were agitated not over the penal code but over jury trial. . . . Juries presume a people as judge, and a people can not judge if it is not enlightened. . . . But in the State of Guatemala there were cultured people worthy of a jury guarantee. Now, one can ask if these people should enjoy neither the jury system nor any of the advantages of modern civilization because great masses of barbarous Indians accept no progress nor aspire to more than the stake? If the Indians are outside of civilization, they are not outside of nature, and human nature does not rebel unless it experiences great harm. . . . the absence of the Archbishop was of no consequence to the Indians; most of them neither knew nor missed him.[32]

The divorce and inheritance laws, although perhaps more socially defensible in their goals, suffered an even worse partisan fate. The law establishing civil marriage also opened the door to divorce. The decree simply stated: "1. The Law considers marriage only a civil contract, and as a consequence it can be rescinded. 2. All those who declare themselves divorced, with the solemnities of Decree 20 of last year (1836), are eligible to enter into a new marriage."[33] Once again, Montúfar explained the resulting furor in partisan terms: "The Indians do not know what civil marriage is, nor are they obliged to marry civilly. . . . Thus, it is impossible to assume that a law whose consequences they did not experience angered them. . . . The persons wounded most dearly were the priests. . . . A strong hand, a few days of dictatorship, would have saved the [Liberal] institutions [from the forces of Carrera]."[34]

The civil matrimony–divorce law was popularly termed the "Dog Law" (*la ley de perro*). This measure, together with one defining the inheritance rights of illegitimate children, purported to defend women and children, whereas its critics denounced it as both heretical and criminally irresponsible. They asserted that it would reduce the sanctity of marriage to the animal kingdom while claiming to defend the rights of the victims of just the sort of behavior it would unleash, if not openly sanction.

Undoubtedly, the Church and opportunistic Conservative politicians both fomented and benefited from the widespread popular reaction against these laws. Nevertheless, why this reaction occurred, beyond clerical manipulations, sheds some light on the dilemmas and failures of the early Liberal secularization policy. Although some Liberal leaders were themselves precisely the sort of illegitimate children intended as beneficiaries of the law, they were just as often those whose behavior was to be restrained or punished. Such a law would have had meaning only in the few urban centers of the time, and one is hard-pressed to determine which side was more hypocritical: the Church in defending the sanctity of a marriage bond that was often financially beyond the reach of most people (see below for further detail on household composition) or the Liberals in pursuing a policy more likely to exaggerate the irresponsible masculine behavior it claimed to restrain. Of more importance, the irrelevance of the entire debate for a commoner society denied participation in the rights being so pompously debated certainly fed into the anger evident in the Church-led opposition to the law.

Only when the social position of most Liberals, outside of the few radicals of Guatemala City, and their similar sociosexual behavior when compared to their Conservative counterparts are recognized can the widespread popular repudiation of these laws be understood. The reaction was ably manipulated by clerics for their own purposes, but their orthodox denunciations alone did not create it. However defensible the initiatives themselves, it was not hard to see that neither oppressed wives nor abandoned children were likely to be its prime beneficiaries. More likely, elite males, both Conservative and Liberal, would have even greater leeway to behave in ways that created the problem being addressed. Although the Conservatives offered little that was constructive in this regard, nonelite society could easily recognize on its own the hypocrisy and superficiality of the solution offered by the Liberals.

Similar attitudes could be seen with regard to the principle of lay versus clerical education. Reacting to visionary Liberal initiatives of June 1830 and March 1832, some clerics and Conservatives took the almost absurd position of opposing any broad education program at all. Indeed, it was not difficult to see why the Liberal revolutionary Ramón Rosa would refer to the Conservative education law of 1852 as "the ill-fated child of the reactionary thought of Sr. Manuel F. Pavón."[35] The so-called Pavón law asserted:

> All good and solid instruction consists in learning the doctrine of our Religion, and in instilling in the youth from the start its principles and the respect due their parents, their elders, and the officials and authorities to whose good works the people owe their well being. . . . Each day, upon entering the school, the child will kneel before the altar and invoke the Patron Saint. . . . the teacher will take care to instill in the children the firm obligation to respect, love, obey, and serve their parents and elders, priests, and higher authorities, who are God's Representatives on earth.[36]

However, in attempting to uproot clerical influence in education, Liberals also, perhaps inevitably, endangered what little access to formal education was available. They simply were unable to deliver an alternative system, superior even in numerical terms in the short run. In Guatemala in as late as 1866, only about eight to nine thousand children attended primary schools, whereas fifty thousand would by 1887.[37] Even in Costa Rica, where lay education developed rapidly, the major advances took place in the 1880s and thereafter, with majority primary school coverage in the Central Valley achieved both for women and the poor by the early twentieth century. Once again, however laudable in the abstract, the early Liberal policy to secularize education threatened to remove one reality without offering a credible substitute.

Perhaps the most perplexing of the Liberal policies for a mass public was that favoring Protestant immigration to develop the region's economy, particularly its desolate Atlantic lowlands. As noted above, this policy clashed with anti-British attitudes of the more radical Liberals and with the obvious territorial conflicts with the same British government that would authorize much of the settlement. In addition, this Liberal call for secular progress was opposed for even more profound reasons that were beyond the vicious antiforeign and dogmatic campaigns led by the Church.

Both Liberal theorists and most foreign immigrants hinted at, or openly espoused, a racist contempt not only for Indians and blacks but also for the mixed-race poor they were intended to lead by example, if not supplant. This attitude hardly made for popular support for such a self-deprecating policy. Moreover, just as in the case of common lands rental, Liberals had a difficult time explaining how private initiative and greed could have suddenly become the only sure route to public virtue. Thomist teachings on the *summum bonum* (the highest good) and the evils of private interest unrestrained had a logical resonance among a centuries-old Catholic peasantry untouched by Liberal theorizing and with no need for "reactionary" or clerical manipulation to bring it to the fore. Here, again, secularization proved to be far easier in terms of Church property and politics and far more difficult when it came to ideas on the appropriate social order.

Not only did Liberalism's policies in Guatemala generate more mass opposition than support, but its marriage of convenience with the Church in El Salvador also alienated many on the left wing. From the beginning of independent life, El Salvador's elite identified itself as both Liberal and anti-Guatemalan. Ironically, a major symbol of the latter was the recurrent demand for a separate bishopric in San Salvador that was independent of Guatemalan ecclesiastical control. The demand was finally granted in 1842, with the appointment of Jorge de Viteri y Ungo as the first bishop. Thereafter, under both Eugenio Aguilar (1846–1848) and Gerardo Barrios (1859–1863), bishops fled or were expelled, but the Church's economic power in El Salvador was never remotely comparable to its counterpart in Guatemala, nor was it the real focus of political strife. The difficulties of developing a secular and anticlerical identity while demanding the appointment of a new "national" bishop tested the rhetorical powers of Salvadoran Liberals, just as had been the case with Arce and his coalition government with Aycinena in the 1820s and the perennial attempts to reconcile the more radical social implications of their ideology with their role as the dominant class in local society. The problems of Gerardo Barrios with the Church cannot hide the fact that secularism as an ideology in El Salvador, given its historical commitment to the national bishopric, was even more elitist than in Guatemala itself.

For early Liberals the inability to develop a series of images, an identity, a discourse capable of galvanizing mass support was a basic problem. In Guatemala serious attempts were made, and they had their echo elsewhere: the Gálvez-era attack on powerful Church symbols and social institutions. Although of real interest to urban, mixed-race groups hopeful of social improvements in their lot, these issues were of little positive interest to the mass of society. Indeed, the issues could readily be countered with a Catholic discourse that appeared more credible or, worse, with a revelation of the internal inconsistencies of such an appeal to embrace foreign models in the name of nationhood. As time went on Liberal ideological appeals became less and less social in their content. Economic progress was more often the promise and the standard of judgment. In effect, the early failures led to a virtual abandonment of a socially radical discourse, to a sort of economic determinism in place of the earlier, romantic call to arms that had repeatedly failed to rouse mass support.

In addition, the Liberals were defeated as much by cholera epidemics as by the Conservatives. Both in 1837–1838 and again in 1856–1857, support of the Liberal program was decimated by epidemic disease. In the first instance the epidemic clearly was exploited by Carrera and the Conservatives for propaganda purposes; they claimed that Gálvez and the Liberals had poisoned the water supply of villages to give over the land to foreign immigrants. Later, the association was far less direct, but Walker's adventure had been identified with a bizarre version of the Liberal program for Central America. More generally, however, epidemic disease appeared as a particularly powerful rejection of Liberal claims for the powers of science and progress. Well past midcentury, Liberal science held no magic for the afflicted. Indeed, the Liberal program had appeared with the messenger of death itself, first in tandem with unintelligible divorce and colonization laws and later with the perfectly intelligible forces of slavery and Anglo-Saxon racism.

Midcentury Liberals offered the masses virtually the antithesis of what would later become the "religion" of science and progress. Instead of promising the wonders of mechanized production and transport, public health, and the "order and progress" designed, consciously or not, to instill in the masses a "modern" awe and respect analogous to the religious symbolism of medieval times, the early Liberals had only their fiery rhetoric and declining military strength. They were poor weapons, indeed, with which to face cholera in the material world and hellfire and damnation in the symbolic one.

A good example of Liberal ideological weakness, and the strength of Catholic imagery, can be seen in Palmer's contrast of President Mora's and Bishop Llorente's addresses to the troops departing to face Walker in Nicaragua. If any Liberal group in Central America was likely to be successful, it was Costa Rica's coffee-enriched secular authorities, and they should have been able to develop an imagery of mass appeal, which indeed they had begun. Nevertheless, even here a pale defense of prosperity and peace, the Liberal program after midcentury, rather than any vision of egalitarian or libertarian change, was offered by Mora:

> The peace, the happy peace that, combined with your laborious perseverance, has so augmented our credit, riches and contentment, is perfidiously

threatened. A gang of outsiders, the scum of all peoples . . . plan to invade Costa Rica to find in our wives and daughters, in our houses and haciendas, gratification for their ferocious passions. . . . I stand by you, completely convinced that . . . all shall gather with me, beneath our free national flag . . . to defend the homeland like we would defend the sacred mother whom we all love.[38]

In contrast, Bishop Llorente paints a far richer canvas of the motherland and its traditions to be defended:

These are the bitter enemies of our sacred religion: What will become of our temples, of our altars, of our law? What will be the fate of our Lord's Anointed? Unleashed in their passions: What can you expect for your chaste wives and innocent daughters? Thirsty for riches: How will you preserve your property? . . . God shall confound them: therefore do not fear them. The God who freed Ananias, Azariah and Mishael from the flames, He that freed Daniel from the lion's den. He shall free you also. . . . Renew your spirit with the exercise of virtue so that in the event that death comes upon us in the defense of our Religion, of our Homeland, of our independence, of our laws, lives and properties, we might have a propitious meeting with the Supreme Judge.[39]

However different in tone and emotive power, both calls were rooted in traditional, Catholic, parochial imagery rather than in the Liberal framework invented by radical Guatemalans in the 1830s. Common to even this classic coffee baron's political discourse were the key images of peace and motherland versus the rape, pillage, and evil brought by the infidel Protestant invaders. Thus, even in Costa Rica, where Liberalism's economic transformations were most advanced, the trial by fire of nationhood was faced with far more of a sense of divine, Biblical testing and eternal communities that were simultaneously religious and political rather than with nationality along secular, Liberal lines.

Society Transformed:
Economic and Demographic Bases

The Liberal challenge foresaw a future Central America vastly altered in its demographic and economic patterns. The future would be one of a Creole-mestizo rather than an Indian majority, a prosperous and exporting rather than a backward and self-sufficient economy. Liberal dreams might

A Judas burning in San José, Costa Rica, 1858 (from Ricardo Fernández Guardia, Costa Rica en el siglo XIX)

have led to radical changes, but the demographic changes were not to become reality. Moreover, Liberal theorists often poorly understood the most basic patterns of the societies they were so determined to transform.

At midcentury Central America remained divided along both ethnic and regional lines. Ethnically, the dividing line was between a densely settled indigenous majority in the north and a mestizo equivalent in the under-populated south. El Salvador was essentially the transition zone in such a dichotomous reality. For all practical purposes the Atlantic watershed of the region was not part of the calculations of political leaders. However, the experience of its sparsely settled inhabitants also will be referred to later when dealing with this issue of ethnic distribution and identity.

Both north and south were characterized by a rural/urban or village/city dichotomy in the highlands and Pacific piedmont, whereas the Pacific coastal plain was virtually one giant cattle range with few urban concentra-

111

tions. These spatial patterns profoundly conditioned demographic, social, and economic developments. Not only was most of the overall population in the north, but the village or rural component of the population was predominant regionwide (Table 6). Nevertheless, although village dwellers depended primarily on agriculture for a livelihood, they did so within a common lands system of considerable nucleation and occupational complexity. Curiously, it was here that Liberal support for export growth would have a great impact, although the Liberals themselves consistently ignored or disparaged the existing social division of labor and regional economic specialization.

During the Bourbon period considerable interregional trade and specialization had developed around the indigo-producing hub of El Salvador. Both Guatemalan and Panamanian merchants benefited from the growing export trade that was fundamentally based on El Salvador's indigo fields. Highland Guatemala produced textiles consumed as far away as Costa Rica, whose merchants made the trip north until at least the early 1840s to acquire their stock. Tobacco and cattle moved north in payment for domestic and foreign trade goods, with the overall system controlled and financed from Guatemala City and Belize.

In 1847, Dunlop described this system on the eve of its disarticulation because of English imports: "About 100,000 dollars, principally in gold coin, are annually received from Costa Rica for the purchase of woolen clothing, made in the Altos, which is generally worn in Costa Rica. The money is always personally brought by the natives of the State, who return with the woolen manufactures which they retail to their countrymen."[40]

With the breakdown of the federation in the late 1830s, and particularly after the development of coffee exports, each of the five republics would develop individual trade networks oriented directly to the English and European markets. The old complementarity and trade routes would fall into disuse, and, as Lindo-Fuentes showed earlier, no central government was able to maintain an ability to tax such a diverse combination of externally oriented trade flows. Lindo-Fuentes also showed how each of the five nations consolidated its state apparatus around the ability to tax these new products and routes and how Costa Rica, El Salvador, and Guatemala were more successful in that attempt than Nicaragua and Honduras.

Clearly, midcentury economic redirection had important political consequences. In addition, it had a major impact on occupational and demographic structures. In surely the most isolated and primitive of the

Table 6. *Estimated Population of Central America, 1820–1870 (in thousands)*

Country	1820	1830	1840	1850	1860	1870
Costa Rica	63	72	86	101	115	137
El Salvador	248	271	315	366	424	493
Guatemala	595	670	751	847	951	1080
Honduras	135	152	178	203	230	265
Nicaragua	186	220	242	274	278	337
Central America	1227	1385	1572	1791	1998	2312

Source: Ralph Lee Woodward, Jr., "Central America," in *Spanish America after Independence, c. 1820–c. 1870,* ed. Leslie Bethell (Cambridge: Cambridge University Press, 1987), 178.

five republics, Costa Rica, these changes can be seen most clearly and dramatically.[41] The earlier village economy, with a substantial social division of labor in an urban, if archaic system, was rapidly transformed. Occupational diversity was radically reduced with the elimination, in a single generation (1840–1870), of a whole class of artisan callings. Rapid movements of population to the coffee-producing frontier or fringe areas led to a society whose labor productivity was substantially greater but who depended on English imports rather than local or regional artisan production.

Elsewhere in Central America these changes came more slowly and less dramatically, but they followed much the same pattern in the long run. Honduras and Nicaragua were the least successful in regard to this Liberal policy, whereas Guatemala, as the largest, most complex society of the five, was less overwhelmed by these new patterns. El Salvador came closest, perhaps, to approximating the model established early by coffee-based Costa Rica: ruralization of economic life; simplification of the direct export trade under local control; occupational homogenization at the expense of colonial artisanry and urban life; and increased labor productivity, trade levels, and wealth that rewarded those who controlled land, capital, and

113

trade most directly but that increased levels of wealth across the board. Although Liberals often painted the bleakest picture of economic primitiveness in contrast to the siren calls of progress, what they were in fact proposing was a radical transformation of a substantially complex colonial economy. If this economy was primitive, then it was so in technology, labor productivity, and external trade, not in occupational distribution or domestic exchange.

In pursuing an export-led growth strategy, those who supported coffee were also to transform the regional population equation. Where in colonial and early independent times the artisan-rich areas of highland Guatemala and León dominated much of regional economic life, their economic role would decline radically with both the collapse of that system and the rise of its coffee-based, European trade–oriented successor. If Granada was León's nemesis, then San Salvador was equally Guatemala City's in this process of realignment. More accurately, the loss of Costa Rica's consumer market to the British trade was the equivalent for León (and Granada) of San Salvador's escape from Guatemalan control, and it was the exchange of raw materials (indigo and coffee) for English trade goods that led the way in each case.

The effects of this reorientation on the one area most devastated by the changes, Los Altos, were described accurately and critically by the local priest, Fernando Antonio Dávila, in 1846, only two years before he would be implicated in the Liberal attempt at insurrection. Reflecting major elements of the Conservative and artisanal critiques of the effects of Liberal free trade policies, Dávila reported:

In 1833 [there were] . . . 278 cotton looms; 150 for wool; . . . this decline [by 1846] is evident, as are its causes. . . . suffice it to list the manufactures introduced from abroad. For example, in regard to cloth, even the white and colored cotton yarn and thread come from abroad; bed covers or blankets; overabundant supplies of cloth, the coarser variety being for the attire of the common people. This short listing shows that the country's industry, in regard to cotton cloth, is nil. Regarding hardware all kinds of nails, lock–smithery, common tools for planting and carpentry, like hoes, machetes, hatchets, saws, and chisels are brought from abroad, such that the iron works of the country are reduced to zero. . . . The only line of manufactures [we had were] in cotton. . . . That is why these same Indian women used to say, in their simple yet forceful and expressive idiom, cotton is our mother, our father. The tariff law favoring the foreigner who brings his cotton yarn and feeble cloth took this important industry away from the country, made

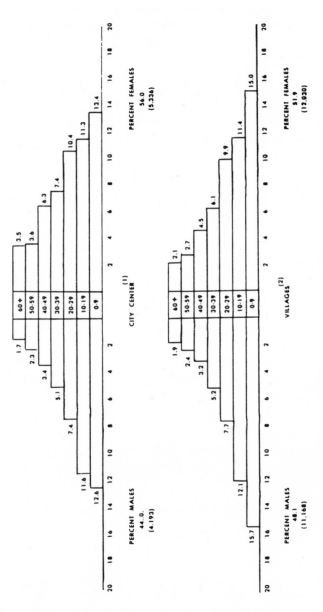

Figure 1. Percent Age Distribution by Sex: City Center versus Villages in Costa Rica, 1844–1846
Sources: Archivos Nacionales de Costa Rica, Gobernación, No. 24,906; Municipal Heredia, No. 481.

(1) City centers of Heredia and Cartago (including Carmen, La Puebla and Guadalupe) in 1846 and 1844 respectively.

(2) Surrounding Villages.

the people dependent on a foreign power, . . . and forced these women, so habitually hardworking from childhood, into abandonment and idleness.[42]

The Central America that awaited export agriculture and its transformations was a mosaic of radically different societies on Atlantic and Pacific coasts and in the volcanic highlands. However, in those areas that began to develop export industries by midcentury—the Pacific piedmont and the lower levels of the volcanic highlands—colonial settlement had led to a basic rural/urban or village/city dichotomy. As Figure 1 shows for midcentury Costa Rica, the village or rural population was somewhat younger, more balanced by gender, and thus characterized by earlier ages of marriage (19–21 for women and 24–26 for men) and somewhat higher growth rates than the city. To the extent that export agriculture ruralized the population, then, growth rates would likely rise and, of more importance, race mixture and Ladino/mestizo homogeneity would become that much more plausible a future to some people.

Relatively little is known yet of the more precise vital rate and human geography characteristics of the midcentury Central American population. Since early colonial times it had been apparent to all that the mixed-race population grew more rapidly than its village Indian equivalent. However, this early difference in growth rates was increasingly less the case over time because Indians came to have the youngest age at first marriage and the lowest rates of celibacy, in part as a consequence of clerical policy aimed particularly at the Indian population.

The Guatemalan highland population developed a highly distinctive pattern of regional trade centers or towns and artisan exchange during this period. It also developed a complex settlement pattern in which kin groups or clans formed outlying settlements (*parcialidades*) dependent on larger indigenous administrative centers. Although this pattern caused many Crown and later national officials to denounce such dispersion as typically barbaric Indian behavior, no particular indigenous character need be imputed to such a general pattern. El Salvador's indigo growers were regularly denounced as irreligious in their dispersed settlement types. Of more importance, in settings as thoroughly Ladino as Costa Rica, village society was profoundly tied to a landholding system tolerant of much the same fragmentation of dwellings in the countryside. Although never as fully developed as the indigenous parcialidad perhaps, the far south developed a pattern of *rincón*, or corner settlement and land claims. Each such area of land surrounding the village site would carry an

116

identifying family/place name (Rincón Alvarez, Zamora, for example), as well as cattle pens and perhaps dwellings of the proprietor clan.

The development of export agriculture increased such tendencies to dispersion as it incorporated vast areas of unsettled land. Nevertheless, village society was not simply "rural" or dispersed, nor was it reducible to the village residential area. Nucleation of residence might remain a general principle of social organization but with it occurred more frequent fissure and establishment of new *rancherías*, or clusters of dwellings, in the process of frontier, village settlement. This emerging pattern of settlement was vividly described, and bemoaned, by Narciso Escobar, the *agrimensor* (land surveyor) charged with the unenviable task of adjudicating the land claims in the emerging coffee fields in the commons of Palmar and Santa María, Quetzaltenango, in the 1870s. He described the area as peppered (*salpicada*) with home and crop sites, including dozens of tiny coffee groves interspersed with various other crops. He despaired of any simple solution because even if all existing claims to plantings were granted, the individual pieces would be so fragmented that none of the beneficiaries would be completely satisfied.[43]

Household organization is only now being studied by researchers, most often within Hispanic (non-Indian) and urban society.[44] One fact is that in midcentury Costa Rica complex and multigenerational households were infrequent within both urban and village contexts. In that country, for example, families headed by a man that had three generations present in the household accounted for only 2 or 3 percent of all households, although the number increased substantially with the later, twentieth-century development of coffee monoculture and land scarcity. Such households were identified with areas of high concentrations of wealth, as in the largest cities, but they never accounted for a major share of households even in San José or Cartago. Although domestic service was widespread, and likely a form of social protection as well as labor, complex and multigenerational households tended to be more frequent among households headed by a woman. Nevertheless, overall such households accounted for only about 25 percent to 35 percent of households in city centers and 15 percent to 25 percent in the villages versus the 25 percent to 50 percent that reported at least one domestic servant.

By far the most frequent household unit, particularly in the villages, was the simple nuclear family, headed either by a father and mother or by a single mother or widow. Overall household size was small, with an average of only two to four children at any one point in time. Women heads of household accounted for anywhere from 15 percent to 20 percent (villages) to 25 percent to 30 percent (cities) of all households, most frequently in areas of high concentrations of wealth and mixed-race populations. However concentrated among urban and poor populations, particularly African-American groups, the female head of household, as well as single motherhood, was a characteristic in every level and group of society to one extent or another.

How much Hispanic society elsewhere conformed to these Costa Rican patterns, not to mention Indian village society, remains unclear. Moreover, disaggregating the data by race, class, and residence (city versus village) awaits further research virtually everywhere in Central America.

The Liberal divorce and inheritance laws were developed within this context of generalized illegitimacy and concubinage in urban, Hispanic society. Perhaps the most telling irony is that found in the Liberals' evolution on the issue of inheritance law. Their first attempt was a socially radical claim to defend the rights of illegitimate children to their biological father's estate. The 1837 decree argued in favor of paternal authority, to be sure, but it also claimed that the exclusion of illegitimate children from their father's estate was a case of false morality that attempted to "uselessly repress and punish in children the disorderliness of their parents." Thus, it held that the freedom to will was absolute as long as property was not left to the Church 'but that illegitimate children, once legally recognized by their fathers, inherited in equal conditions with legitimate ones.[45]

By the 1870s the triumphant Liberals only wanted to free the patriarch to dispose of his property with as few restrictions as possible. President Justo Rufino Barrios explained this change in policy:

> Whereas: The freedom to will within the family favors its interests, strengthening the head of the family's authority. The father knows best the family's needs and interests; it is right and just that he be free to dispose of his goods. . . . The intervention of the Law in matters such as these is improper and prejudicial to the authority of the father, who is the best judge of his family's interests, and chosen by his natural sentiments to seek the well being of his descendants, to reward or punish their deeds. . . . The existing laws on the investigation of paternity present, in their latitude, several obstacles which must be avoided; therefore, I decree:
>
> Article 1. Parents and forebearers may freely dispose of their goods among their legitimate descendants. . . .
>
> Article 3. The food allowance of the illegitimate children deprived of

118

inheritance may not exceed that which would have corresponded to them if their father had distributed his goods equally among [all] his children.

Article 4. The food allowance of "natural" [paternally recognized but not the product of a Church-sanctioned marriage] children may not exceed one-fifth of the estate in cases where legitimate descendants exist.[46]

The radical Liberals had allowed their policy goals, however socially leveling, to become confused with means likely to aggravate an arbitrary and irresponsible patriarchal behavior, and the second-generation Liberals disavowed the former while feigning ignorance of the latter. Gone was any reform agenda seeking social equality, however misguided in its means. Illegitimate and, more frequently, mixed-race children were reconfirmed in their centuries-old position as second-class heirs and citizens, provided their father legally recognized them. Even then, their ability to press inheritance claims was limited essentially to a maintenance allowance when legitimate children existed.

Where colonial standards required provision for all legitimate heirs and basic partibility unless a *mayorazgo* (indivisible estate) was being founded, the second-generation Liberals struck down, in the name of the economic and patriarchal freedom of action they held most dear, most such limitations in this area of deathbed private initiative. At least in Costa Rica it is clear that the pattern of inheritance was not radically altered in practice by these new legal freedoms.[47] Nevertheless, perhaps no clearer example might be found of the fading social and looming economic agendas of Liberalism during the period 1840–1870. Its change of heart on this issue, unlike many other areas, did involve matters of the heart as well as political economy.

The patriarchal authoritarianism of second-generation Liberals can be seen more generally in their attitudes toward women outside of traditional roles. The heirs to Liberal triumph, distinguished jurists such as Rafael Pineda Mont, took radically different positions compared with the doctrinaire or romantic Liberals of the federation era. In his 1894 graduation thesis on the once-conflictive topic of the justifications for divorce, Pineda Mont argued vehemently that no such grounds existed.[48] His fellow student, José Flores Flores, argued that no legal means should be provided for investigations of paternity and stated: "Gentlemen, paternity is a fact shrouded in obscurity, in mystery; the Law can not firmly and securely penetrate there; and if it attempts to decide what the very mother may ignore, it opens itself to making grave mistakes, which is why marriage has been established. . . . Allowing judgements of paternity and blood ties is to right one wrong by substituting others."[49]

Their contemporaries in power, less concerned with theoretical niceties, made use of police power and concerns regarding public health to institute what amounted to state-regulated prostitution in the capital.[50] Once again, freedom and the market were ultimate goods and goals but only within the comfortable boundaries of patriarchy and property.

Society Redefined: Race Mixture and Ethnic Identity

Ethnic classification in nineteenth-century Central America, as before and after that period, was as much a political statement and fiscal category as any kind of biological assessment of parentage. In colonial times Indians were those who paid head and labor taxes as members of recognized Indian communities, regardless of biological heritage. Those who did not were not Indians, once again "race" notwithstanding. After independence, Indians were those who identified themselves as such through speech, dress, and village membership and, of more importance, engaged in largely subsistence agriculture on village or common lands. To the extent that some Indians undertook to privatize landownership or to grow export crops, some thought they saw the beginnings of a miraculous racial transformation. As one midcentury Salvadoran Hispanic observer put it:

> It can be said that among us the Indian race is disappearing. . . . We have seen that practically each Indian who has converted, so to speak, to the Spanish race, has become a hard working agriculturalist or an intelligent artisan. . . . Those who years back were called Indians, who had occupations appropriate to beasts of burden and who only produced maize and beans, are now ladinos, and occupy themselves in the cultivation of sugar cane, coffee, tobacco, and other things more important than maize and beans.[51]

Only the most general impressions of the ethnic makeup of Central America can be offered. In Petén, Verapaz, and Los Altos in Guatemala, more than 75 percent to 95 percent of the population was considered Indian. However, in the area surrounding Guatemala City to the southwest and east, between one-half and two-thirds were non-Indian or Ladino. In the provinces from El Salvador to Nicaragua, the Indian component of the population ranged from one-quarter to one-half, declining as one moved south. In Costa Rica, perhaps 75 percent to 95 percent of the population was non-Indian, although they were not as Spanish or European in genetic background as traditionally thought.

Outside of Guatemala City little in the way of European-born population existed, and thus little of the peninsular/Creole conflict that occurred at elite levels of society was seen. This lack of European population also led to the inclusion of many light-skinned individuals of recognizably mixed race among the ranks of white society, especially in the provinces. Social class and shared culture proved far more important in cementing elite unity than any racist hairsplitting, although many cases of attempted discrimination against individual enemies might be found. The passing of the mixed-race wealthy into the ranks of white society through marriage is easily documented and was commented on by local and foreign observers throughout the period. Political rivals in midcentury Costa Rica ridiculed each other as *zambos* and *canacos* (swarthy, Polynesian complexion), and the German visitor Marr disparaged President Mora as an anemic Indian. More pointedly, perhaps, Dionisio Herrera, the Honduran appointed president of Nicaragua by Morazán in 1829, was frequently mocked by his opponents as part African or mulatto, and much of that country's political difficulty was ascribed by regional critics to its alleged zambo or mulatto indiscipline and violent nature.

The question of the position of the mixed races within the Hispanic republic (mixed-race village Indians remained Indians for all intents and purposes) was as much political as racial. Many modern authors have wrongly assumed that the answer to this question was biologically or vaguely culturally based. In fact, as with any such inherently ambiguous ethnic classification, the categories used had relatively little to do with race and much more to do with position. One's race was fundamentally an expression of the oppositional characteristics, politically and behaviorally, of an individual compared with social superiors and inferiors.

Carol Smith has argued that the ubiquitous term "Ladino" in Guatemala acquired a new, socially specific meaning with the development of coffee culture in the post-1870 period. In effect, she argues that Ladinos were "(re)invented" as a social category as part of the triumph of coffee and Liberalism.[52] Thereafter, Ladino would mean someone presumably of mixed race, fully Hispanic culturally, entitled to an escape from forced Indian labor, and potentially deserving of a share in its exploitation (as a foreman, labor recruiter, loan shark, or *pulpero* [grocer], for example).

This argument should not be overstated. Ladinos clearly existed before coffee culture and were thus named, whatever the meaning of the term at

Coffee and Ethnicity. Above: The New Rich and European Fashion, Hacienda Serijiers, Guatemala, 1875. Below: Indian Harvesters, San Isidro, Guatemala, 1875 (Photos from Edweard Muybridge, Central America Album, *courtesy of the Boston Atheneum)*

122

any given time. However, the basic pattern, that of the changing, political basis of ethnic terminology, also can be seen in earlier periods. During much of the colonial period "mestizo" was a term reserved for the more socially meritorious, as in *mestizo legítimo*, accentuating the presumably legitimate Spanish parentage involved. Similarly, "mulatto" usually was used to describe populations who were often of virtually identical mixed race but whose position was either lower on the social scale or characterized by insubordination in settlement type, labor/tax obligations, or domestic arrangements.

During the late colonial and early independent periods, the Salvadoran mixed-race population of poquitero indigo producers and seasonal hacienda workers was regularly referred to as mulatto.[53] They received this baptism in the same breath as the elite authors involved lamented their dispersed, illegal settlements in *valles* (valleys) and *realengas* (untitled royal lands) and the difficulty in extracting labor or religious devotion from them. Thus, three of the major labels assigned to mixed races—Ladino, mestizo, and mulatto—had clearly sociopolitical connotations beyond any racial heritage scheme, and these meanings changed over time. Furthermore, the term "zambo" (Indian/African) was nearly always used in reference to the zambo/mosquitos, a clearly political and military statement with little or no pretense to any objective basis in race. The dangers of exaggeration are equally great here perhaps, but it is indeed striking that mixed races are more frequently described as mulattoes when a critical, lamenting tone is being adopted, as in the indigo-based conflicts of El Salvador, the complaints of Guatemalan elites heard early in independence regarding provincial and lower class insubordination ("anarchy"), or whenever the "lethargy" of cattle ranch hands is bemoaned by foreign or local elite observers.

Beyond the political nature of ethnic classification, it is important to remember both that the African component of the Ladino, mixed races was much greater than commonly thought (likely greater, in fact, than the Hispanic contribution) and that it could "disappear" as part of the general process of race mixture, whitening, and passing so typical of the increasingly homogeneous Hispanic republic. Lutz has shown how early colonial Santiago was actually more African-American than European-American.[54] Similarly, the vast Pacific plains of Central America, once they were almost completely emptied of native population because of disease, were given over to nearly wild cattle herds tended by the mulatto and zambo descendants of African slave cowboys imported for this specialized occupation.

Society and Politics

This increasing mixed-race homogeneity and the evident social cohesion of the Hispanic republic were the results both of the mixed races' recognized vulnerability, as isolated ships in a sea of potentially hostile Indian communities, and of the pattern of race mixture promoted at all social levels. Hispanic society, although it did not formally encourage race mixture, especially with regard to Africans, promoted it by powerful socioeconomic, demographic, and intellectual forces. In any society that rewards those of lighter skin with better life chances, whitening in the selection of mating and marriage partners will likely result. This result was certainly the case in Hispanic Central America. Moreover, given the chronic imbalance between the sexes for both European Americans and African Americans (male predominance in the countryside; female in the cities), rapid race mixture became that much more likely.[55] Finally, the favored economic position of many African-American males in the Indian countryside and their understandable desire for free-born rather than slave children led to the growth of the mulatto/zambo population and its whitening over time.

Whitening and white supremacy were the largely unquestioned, and in any case unquestionable, norms of Hispanic Central America. However, on its periphery some unique variations on this theme were to develop. In areas such as Petén and the Mosquito coast, locally dominant groups made much of their nonindigenous heritage but with substantially different concrete identities. On the far north (Petén) and south (Talamanca), Hispanic settlement was so limited and fragile that indigenous society suffered little direct pressure. There Hispanics were essentially the mestizo descendants of adventurer/settler groups whose basic (only?) differences vis-à-vis natives were their cattle herds, frustrated desires for export-generated wealth, and pretensions to labor services. In such isolation, little could be gained in the name of Hispanic civilization. Here, race mixture continued but without whitening, and the small Hispanic community had to content itself with a largely cultural and economic distinctiveness, zealously expressed in elaborate genealogies, rather than any visibly racial one.

On the Mosquito coast an even more distinctive ethnic process of change was taking shape. From the mid-seventeenth century forward the term "zambo-mosquito" was coined to highlight, from the Spanish viewpoint, the African heritage of the coastal peoples. The English, on the contrary, chose to emphasize the presumably more legitimate Indian heritage and territorial claims, crowning several indigenous "Kings of the

Mosquitia." However, as trade and logging activities with Jamaican and North American agents increased during the nineteenth century, those who came to manipulate the successive kings were less often British officials and more often the so-called Creoles of the coast. Most notably beginning with the Shepherd brothers in the early independent period, these light-skinned mulattoes from Jamaica came to dominate the coastal trading network and Mosquito royalty. In this context, ethnicity once again expressed relationships of social and political power, but the expression occurred within a framework of Creole or mulatto superiority and indigenous inferiority, rather than the familiar three-part (white Hispanic/Ladino/Indian) system of the highlands and Pacific plain.

Just as in the case of the twentieth-century Atlantic coast and as Smith suggests for earlier, coffee-based society, would-be ethnic categories serve as social markers rather than as reminders of biological "facts." What Philippe Bourgois, an interpreter of the Central American Atlantic coastal society in more recent times, has termed "conjugated oppression" by class and race appears to have characterized the entire region from the beginnings of colonial rule.[56] However, the precise grammar and syntax of this conjugation and the ethnic terms it uses have varied substantially by both time and place. Indeed, "white civilization" could be menaced by mulatto insubordination in the indigo fields of El Salvador, whereas they were its bearers and defenders both in the cattle ranges of Nicaragua and Costa Rica and on the Mosquito coast. Although the logic of whitening remained the same, its supporters and victims appeared in a kaleidoscope of combinations throughout the region. As elsewhere in Latin America, race was the idiom of invidious distinction for the socially powerful far more than the literal basis for that power. This socially grounded logic of conflict made for the most illogical uses of racial and ethnic terminology by which to express itself.

Conclusion

The social and political tragedies that were to follow the Liberal triumph of the 1870s in northern Central America already could be partially discerned in the period of Conservative ascendancy. Liberal inadequacies, far from being redressed, were actually solidified; vices became partisan, ideological virtues. If the Indian masses did not comprehend, then they must be silenced in the name of progress. If the popular classes in general

Mosquito Chief Robert Henry Clarence (seated, center) with his executive council, 1893; all the council members were of Jamaican descent. (Popular Science Monthly, vol. 45, no. 6, June 1894)

clung to a communitarian Catholicism and were unmoved by secular appeals, then mass education would require (Liberal) dictatorship rather than simply undermining its Conservative form. If the poor supported Conservative-led xenophobia, then only the most direct collaboration with foreign investment interests would solve the political equation for Liberals. If personalized despotism was to be removed once and for all, then Liberal unity was required above all else, leading to a new form of the same old problem: *continuismo* (extending the stay in power by whatever means necessary) and *personalismo* (personalism in its more extreme and charismatic [often dictatorial] form). If Gálvez, the great leader of early Liberalism, could reelect himself twice in processes of dubious legitimacy, then why should heroes of the new age limit themselves in the face of even greater challenges?

Perhaps the greatest tragedy of triumphant Liberalism was the distortion of its two great contributions to nineteenth-century political life: opposition to dictatorship and a larger role for new groups of lesser social standing in Ladino society. The inability of Liberals outside of Costa Rica to reach a modus vivendi with their political opponents—as distinct from the frequent practice of receiving with open arms former Conservatives as part of a Liberal, single-party state—led, in the twentieth century, to some of the most primitive, bizarre, and bloody dictatorships of modern times, whether led by military figures or Liberal civilian politicians convinced of their indispensability. Liberalism's legacy here was far from what one might expect from a doctrine based on the "Rights of Man" and "the Citizen." Despite its youthful infatuation with French revolutionary imagery, nineteenth-century Central American Liberalism was rarely characterized by an acute awareness of its minoritarian, elitist nature. Indeed, for some this ignorance became a virtue of sorts, whether as enlightened rebels out to destroy Conservative bigotry and obscurantism early, or as the self-appointed high priests of progress and the religion of science nearer century's end.

In the social and economic realms also, Liberal triumph had some surprising outcomes. As Pérez Brignoli has noted, to a large extent the second-generation Liberals of Central America consolidated themselves as an economic class simultaneously with their seizure of political power.[57] However, in the context of their weak economic and minoritarian social status, the Hispanic or Ladino petty bourgeoisie of coffee growers and merchants brought to a larger share of political power after the 1870s proved less capable of creating a bourgeois democracy than of striking alliances with their former enemies among the traditionally wealthy and with foreign investors, whether North American, British, or German.

Why did these potentially petty bourgeois revolutions prove so empty in northern Central America? The answer to this question can be found in the peculiar social and economic structure of Central America during the Conservative interlude of the mid-nineteenth century. From the beginning, the critical mass of partisan Liberalism was not to be found in aspiring middle classes or petty bourgeoisie. It was every bit as landed, and nearly as elitist, as its Conservative enemy, particularly in the provinces. New money and blood might dispute old money and quasi-nobility, but money and personal political dominance remained the basic pattern and goal. Coffee's success would accelerate the rise to power of a new Liberal leadership and program, but the radical urban and artisanal elements within the movement were not to dominate it. Indeed, radical Liberalism's influence would linger into the early twentieth century, but it just as often was in opposition to the official variety as it supported it.

Society and Politics

Triumphant export producers in a bitterly divided countryside had much in common with the Conservatives they soon embraced (in private of course). This embrace was not the first such connection, however. Midcentury Conservatives had pardoned earlier Liberal "excesses" and had found common ground on the issue of export promotion. It was that first marriage of convenience that helped bring the Liberals back to power in the 1870s to carry out a revolution that never was. When they faced enemies the likes of "barbaric" mulattoes and Indians in the countryside, opponents tailor-made to fit the needs of any proponent of land privatization, their reactionary policies were hardly surprising. However dramatic and brutal the consequences of the Liberal reforms of the 1870s and thereafter, their oligarchic tendencies should come as no surprise to those familiar with the Conservative interlude that preceded them.

Notes

1. This classic characterization of the early independent period in Hispanic America was made by Tulio Halperín Donghi in his *Historia contemporánea de América Latina* (Madrid: Alianza Editorial, 1970); and *The Aftermath of Revolution in Latin America*, trans. Josephine de Bunsen (New York: Harper, 1973).

2. Pedro Cortés y Larraz, *Descripción geográfico-moral de la diocesis de Goathemala*, Biblioteca Goathemala, vol. 20, tomo 1 (Guatemala: Tipografía Nacional, 1958), 11–14.

3. The long historiographical tradition glorifying the Liberal revolutions and disparaging Carrera and the Conservatives was challenged in Guatemala primarily by Manuel Coronado Aguilar, "El General Carrera ante la historia," *Anales de la academia de geografía e historia* (Guatemala) 28 (1965): 217–61; and in the United States by Ralph Lee Woodward, "Social Revolution in Guatemala: The Carrera Revolt," in *Applied Enlightenment: Nineteenth Century Liberalism, 1830–1839*, ed. Margaret A. L. Harrison and Robert Wauchope, Middle American Research Institute, no. 23 (New Orleans: Tulane University, 1971), 43–70. Marxist authors such as Severo Martínez Peláez and his classic *La patria del criollo* (San José, Costa Rica: EDUCA, 1972) accept much of the Liberal framework in which little of importance took place from independence to 1871, however much they denounce the Liberal innovations thereafter. For an excellent discussion of the relationships among various historiographic and ideological positions in Guatemala that has great relevance for the rest of Central America, see Carol Smith, "Ideologías de la historia social," *Mesoamérica* 14 (1987): 355–66.

4. Subsequently, authors such as E. Bradford Burns, *The Poverty of Progress: Latin America in the Nineteenth Century* (Berkeley: University of California Press, 1980), heroized the earlier villain as the leader of a "popular" government

defensive of "the folk" in general and the Indian majority in particular. The first detailed study of Carrera was conducted by Hazel M. B. Ingersoll, "The War of the Mountain: A Study of Reactionary Peasant Insurgency in Guatemala, 1837–1873" (Ph.D. diss., George Washington University, 1972). The definitive biography is by Ralph Lee Woodward, *Rafael Carrera and the Emergence of the Republic of Guatemala* (Athens: University of Georgia Press, 1993).

5. Frank Safford, "Bases for Political Alignment in Early Independent Spanish America," in *New Perspectives in Latin American History*, ed. Richard Graham (Austin: University of Texas Press, 1978), 71–111.

6. The expression comes from the work by Rodolfo Cerdas Cruz, *Formación del Estado en Costa Rica* (San José, Costa Rica: Editorial de la Universidad de Costa Rica, 1964; 2nd ed., San José, Costa Rica: Editorial Costa Rica, 1978), 65–72.

7. Pedro Tobar Cruz, *Los montañeses: La facción de los lucíos* (Guatemala: Editorial Universitaria, 1971), 187–88, citing J. Santacruz Noriega, *Gobierno del Capitán General D. Miguel García Granados* (Guatemala: Delgado Impresos, 1979), 24.

8. Numerous examples of these conflicts are detailed by Mario Rodríguez, *A Palmerstonian Diplomat in Central America, Frederick Chatfield, Esq.* (Tucson: University of Arizona Press, 1964); and William Griffiths, *Empires in the Wilderness: Foreign Colonization and Development in Guatemala, 1834–1844* (Chapel Hill: University of North Carolina Press, 1965).

9. I am grateful to Arturo Taracena for pointing out that, even in the successful revolt of 1871, the triumphant forces of Los Altos under Justo Rufino Barrios were not referred to as the Liberals at all but rather as the Army of the West (Ejercito de Occidente). For additional details on Los Altos Liberalism in the 1840s see Taracena, "Estado de los Altos, indígenas y régimen conservador: Guatemala, 1838–1851," in *Avances de Investigación*, Centro de Investigaciones Históricas, no. 64 (San José, Costa Rica: Universidad de Costa Rica, 1993); and "El desarrollo económico y las fronteras de Guatemala: el Estado de los Altos, 1770–1838," in Centro de Estudios Urbanos y Regionales [CEUR], *Territorio y sociedad en Guatemala: Tres ensayos históricos* (Guatemala: Ediciones CEUR, Universidad de San Carlos, 1991).

10. Defensa de Guatemala y su política, no. 2 (Guatemala: Imprenta de la Paz, 1849); located in the César Brañas Library of the Universidad de San Carlos, Miscelánea no. 3352, pp. 2–3.

11. Lorenzo Montúfar, *Memorias autobiográficas* (San José, Costa Rica: Editorial Libro Libre, 1988), 122–23.

12. *El popular* (Quetzaltenango), December 4, 1839; cited in Ralph Lee Woodward, Jr., "The State and the Indian in Conservative Guatemala, 1838–1871" (paper presented at the Annual Meeting of the Latin American Studies Association, New Orleans, March 17–19, 1988), 10, note 19.

13. José Coronel Urtecho, *Reflexiones sobre la historia de Nicaragua (De Gainza a Somoza), Volume II* (Managua: Imprenta Hospicio, 1962), 214–23, 233.

14. Biographical material on Francisco Dueñas comes from Diego Rodríguez, *Artículos políticos del Doctor Francisco Dueñas, Ex-Presidente de la República (precedidos de una biografía)* (San Salvador: Dutriz Hermanos Editores, Tipografía La Unión, 1905), copy held by the César Brañas Library in Guatemala City.

15. Taracena, "Estado de los Altos," 20.

16. Lists of Conservative converts to the Liberal cause can be found in Enrique del Cid Fernández, "Humorismo, sátira y resentimiento conservadores hacia los Jefes de la Revolución de 1871, y la Nueva Sociedad," *Anales de la sociedad de geografía e historia de Guatemala* 43 (1970): 1–4, 129–49; 132, 135.

17. Jerónimo Pérez, *Obras históricas completas* (Managua: Banco de América, 1975), 500–502. *Serviles* here means "the servile," *desnudos* means "the naked," *mechudos* means "longhairs," and *timbucos* means "big bellies"; we think *calandracas* means "grasshoppers."

18. The first to highlight this seeming departure from Carrera's presumably conservative and antiexport policies on the part of Cerna was Wayne Clegern in his essay, "Transition from Conservatism to Liberalism in Guatemala, 1865–1871," in *Hispanic American Essays in Honor of Max Leon Moorehead*, ed. W. Coker (Pensacola, Fla.: Perdido Bay Press, 1979), 98–110. Also see Wayne Clegern, *Origins of Liberal Dictatorship in Central America: Guatemala, 1865–1873* (Boulder: University Press of Colorado, 1994), for update and amplification.

19. For synthetic treatments of Central American coffee economies and their diverse histories see Ciro Cardoso, "Central America: The Liberal Era, c. 1870–1930," in *The Cambridge History of Latin America, Volume V*, ed. Leslie Bethell (London: Cambridge University Press, 1986), 197–227; and Robert Williams, *States and Social Evolution: Coffee and the Formation of National Governments in Central America* (Chapel Hill: University of North Carolina Press, 1994).

20. Law no. 27 of January 19, 1824, sec. 21, Central American Political Ephemera Collection, no. 20, box 2, folder 10, Tulane University Library, New Orleans.

21. Mariano Rivera Paz, César Brañas Library, Miscelánea No. 9911 (January 12, 1836), 47.

22. Robert Dunlop, *Travels in Central America* (London: Longman, Brown, Green and Longman, 1847), 301.

23. Miles Wortman, *Government and Society in Central America* (New York: Columbia University Press, 1982), 237.

24. Carol Smith, "Local History in Global Context: Social and Economic Transitions in Western Guatemala," *Comparative Studies in Society and History* 26 (1984): 193–228.

25. J. R. Barrios, in R. Pineda Mont, *Recopilación de las leyes emetidas por el Gobierno de la República de Guatemala del 3 de junio de 1871 hasta el 30 de junio de 1881, Tomo I* (Guatemala: Imprenta de la Paz, 1881), 3–6.

26. Julio Castellanos Cambranes, *Coffee and Peasants: The Origins of the Modern Plantation Economy in Guatemala, 1853–1897* (Stockholm: Institute of Latin American Studies, 1985); and Héctor Lindo-Fuentes, *Weak Foundations: The Economy of*

Notes

El Salvador in the Nineteenth Century (Berkeley: University of California Press, 1990).

27. Rafael Menjívar, *Acumulación originaria y el desarrollo del capitalismo en El Salvador* (San José, Costa Rica: EDUCA, 1980); David Browning, *El Salvador: Landscape and Society* (London: Clarendon Press, 1971).

28. Juan Carlos Solórzano, "Centroamérica a finales del dominio español," in *Historia general de Centroamérica, volume III*, ed. Héctor Pérez Brignoli (Madrid: Editorial Siruela, 1992); Lorenzo Montúfar, *Reseña histórica de Centroamérica, Tomo I* (Guatemala: Tipografía El Progreso, 1878), 241–45; David McCreery, *Rural Guatemala, 1760–1940* (Stanford: Stanford University Press, forthcoming, chap. 3, note 140).

29. Montúfar, *Reseña histórica, Tomo I*, 274–75.

30. For details on this episode, see Carlos Meléndez Chaverri, *Dr. José María Montealegre* (San José, Costa Rica: Editorial Costa Rica, 1968), 37–69; Lowell Gudmundson, *Hacendados, precaristas y políticos: La ganadería y el latifundismo guanacasteco, 1800–1950* (San José, Costa Rica: Editorial Costa Rica, 1983), 37–42.

31. Tobar Cruz, *Los montañeses*, 125–27, discusses Carrera's alleged economic interests and personal implication in the political assassinations that led to the Lucío revolt. He quotes the Liberal leader José Francisco Barrundia as claiming that Carrera's consort ("the monster's shrewish woman") provoked the violence by monopolizing sales of scarce food grains in the region.

32. Montúfar, *Reseña histórica, Tomo II*, 293–94.

33. Ibid., 344, citing the law of April 10, 1837.

34. Ibid., 346.

35. Ramón Rosa, "Estudios sobre Instrucción Pública" (Guatemala: n.p., 1874), César Brañas Library, Miscelánea no. 3358, document 2, p. 11.

36. Ibid., document 12, pp. 23–24.

37. Steven Palmer, "A Liberal Discipline: Inventing Nations in Guatemala and Costa Rica, 1870–1900" (Ph.D. diss., Columbia University, 1990), 111.

38. Ibid., 74–75.

39. Ibid.

40. Dunlop, *Travels in Central America*, 309.

41. For more detailed analysis of Costa Rican occupational and social change with mid-nineteenth-century coffee culture, see Lowell Gudmundson, *Costa Rica Before Coffee: Society and Economy on the Eve of the Export Boom* (Baton Rouge: Louisiana State University Press, 1986), 43–80.

42. Fernando Antonio Dávila, *Bosquejo del Curato de Quetzaltenango por el cura encargado de la misma parroquia* (Guatemala: Imprenta de la Paz, 1846), César Brañas Library, Miscelánea no. 2820, pp. 29–30, 34.

43. Archivo General de Centroamérica (Guatemala), Ministerio de Gobernación, Legajo 28,645, expediente 654 (1874).

44. The discussion of household composition in Costa Rica comes from

Gudmundson, *Costa Rica Before Coffee*, 120–63. Recent work on family structure in Guatemala and Costa Rica includes Norbert Ortmayr, "Matrimonio, Estado y sociedad en Guatemala (siglo XIX y XX)," in Centro de Estudios Urbanos y Regionales [CEUR], *Territorio y sociedad en Guatemala: Tres ensayos históricos* (Guatemala: Ediciones CEUR, Universidad de San Carlos, 1991); and Eugenia Rodríguez Sáenz, "Padres e hijos: Familia y mercado matrimonial en el Valle Central de Costa Rica (1821–1850)," in *Héroes al gusto y libros de moda: Sociedad y cambio cultural en Costa Rica (1750–1900)*, ed. Iván Molina and Steven Palmer (San José, Costa Rica: Editorial Porvenir, 1992), 45–76.

45. Montúfar, *Reseña histórica, Tomo II*, 347.

46. J. R. Barrios, decree no. 240, July 28, 1879, in Pineda Mont, *Recopilación de las leyes, Tomo I*, 280–81.

47. For results of an analysis of inheritance patterns in Costa Rica in this period, see Lowell Gudmundson, "Peasant, Farmer, Proletarian: Class Formation and Inheritance in a Smallholder Coffee Economy, 1850–1950," *Hispanic American Historical Review* 69 (1989): 221–57.

48. Rafael Pineda Mont h., "Causas legítimas de divorcio; y en qué concepto podrá aceptarse el mutuo consentimiento para obtener su declaratoria," Tesis de Derecho (law thesis) (Guatemala: Tipografía Sánchez y De Guise, 1894), César Brañas Library, Miscelánea no. 3580, document 6.

49. José Flores Flores, "¿Será o no conveniente permitir las indigaciones acerca de la paternidad y filiación de los hijos ilegítimos?" Tesis de Derecho (Guatemala: Tipografía La Unión, n.d.), César Brañas Library, Miscelánea no. 3580, doc. 3.

50. David McCreery, "Una vida de miseria y vergüenza: prostitución femenina en la ciudad de Guatemala, 1880–1920," *Mesoamérica* 7 (1986): 35–60.

51. Lindo-Fuentes, *Weak Foundations*, 172, citing *La Gaceta* (El Salvador), August 3, 1855.

52. Carol A. Smith, "Origins of the National Question in Guatemala: A Hypothesis," in *Guatemalan Indians and the State, 1540 to 1988*, ed. Carol A. Smith (Austin: University of Texas Press, 1990), 72–95.

53. José Antonio Fernández, "To Color All the World Blue: The Indigo Boom and the Central American Market" (Ph.D. diss., University of Texas at Austin, 1992).

54. Christopher Lutz, *Historia sociodemográfica de Santiago de Guatemala, 1541–1773*, Serie Monográfica no. 2 (Antigua: Centro de Investigaciones Regionales de Mesoamérica [CIRMA], 1982).

55. Lowell Gudmundson, "Black into White in Nineteenth-Century Spanish America: Afro-American Assimilation in Argentina and Costa Rica," *Slavery and Abolition* 5 (1984): 35–49.

56. Philippe Bourgois, *Ethnicity at Work: Divided Labor on a Central American Banana Plantation* (Baltimore: Johns Hopkins University Press, 1989).

57. Héctor Pérez-Brignoli, *A Brief History of Central America* (Berkeley: University of California Press, 1989), 94.

Suggestions for Further Reading

General Works

The reader in search of a succinct introduction to Central American political history in this period may consult Ralph Lee Woodward, Jr., "Central America," in *Spanish America after Independence, c. 1820–1870*, ed. Leslie Bethell (London: Cambridge University Press, 1987), 171–206. Any list of classic works on Central American social evolution might begin with the insightful and influential essays by Edelberto Torres-Rivas, *Interpretación del desarrollo social centroamericano* (San José, Costa Rica: Editorial Universitaria Centroamericana [EDUCA], 1971), translated and updated as *History and Society in Central America* (Austin: University of Texas Press, 1993); and Severo Martínez Peláez, *La patria del criollo: Ensayo de interpretación de la realidad colonial guatemalteca* (San José, Costa Rica: EDUCA, 1972). Another classic, if dated, synthesis is the university-level text by Ciro F. S. Cardoso and Héctor Pérez Brignoli, *Centroamérica y la economía occidental, 1520– 1930* (San José: Editorial Universidad de Costa Rica, 1977). In the same category are works by Franklin D. Parker, *The Central American Republics* (London: Oxford University Press, 1964); and Mario Rodríguez, *Central America* (Englewood Cliffs, N.J.: Prentice Hall, 1965). More recent survey histories include Ralph Lee Woodward, Jr., *Central America: A Nation Divided* (New York: Oxford University Press, 2nd ed., 1985); and Héctor Pérez Brignoli, *A Brief History of Central America* (Berkeley: University of California Press, 1989). Among the old classics heavily influenced by Liberal interpretations are Hubert Howe Bancroft, *History of Central America* (San Francisco: The History Company, 1887); and José Antonio Cevallos, *Recuerdos salvadoreños* (San Salvador: Dirección General de Publicaciones, 1965).

Relatively few monographic works cover the entire region, but in addition to those few a handful of studies exist whose findings are so central to an understanding of the region that they deserve to be highlighted from the start. They include Nancy Farriss' work on the Yucatán Maya, *Maya Society under Colonial Rule: The Collective Enterprise of Survival* (Princeton: Princeton University Press, 1984); and Carol Smith's edited collection, *Guatemalan Indians and the State: 1540 to 1988* (Austin: University of Texas Press, 1990). Miles Wortman's study, *Government and Society in Central America, 1680–1840* (New York: Columbia University Press, 1982), attempts to deal with the entire region, although its focus is decidedly Guatemalan/Salvadoran. Three recent works that deal exclusively with Guatemala are also key to an understanding of the larger Central American context in this period. They are: Ralph Lee Woodward, Jr., *Rafael Carrera and the Emergence of the Republic of Guatemala* (Athens: University of Georgia Press, 1993); David McCreery, *Rural Guatemala, 1760–1940* (Stanford: Stanford University Press, forthcoming); and Daniele Pomejano, *Centroamérica: La crisis dell'ancien regime (Guatemala 1840–1870)* (Messina, Italy: By the author, 1990).

Travelers' Accounts

Travelers' accounts are a key source for this lightly studied and poorly understood period. A good place to start is Franklin Parker, ed., *Travels in Central America, 1821–1840* (Gainesville: University Presses of Florida, 1970), which includes selections from the earliest independence-era travelers and a detailed guide to the contents of each account. Full-length works by travelers such as the following can still make profitable reading today: John L. Stephens, *Incidents of Travel in Central America, Chiapas, and Yucatán*, 2 vols. (New York: Harper and Bros., 1841); Orlando W. Roberts, *Narrative of Voyages and Excursions on the East Coast and in the Interior of Central America* (Edinburgh: Constable, 1827; Gainesville: University of Florida Press, 1965); Thomas Young, *Narrative of a Residence on the Mosquito Shore* (London: Smith, Elder, 1842); George Thompson, *Narrative of an Official Visit to Guatemala from Mexico* (London: John Murray, 1829); Henry Dunn, *Guatimala, or, The United Provinces of Central America in 1827–28* (New York: G. & C. Carvill, 1828); Jacobus Haefkens, *Viaje a Guatemala y Centroamérica (1827–1828)* (Guatemala: Editorial Guatemala, 1969); John Hale, *Six Months Residence and Travels in Central America* (New York: W. Borrodaile, 1826); George Washington Montgomery, *Narrative of a Journey to Guatemala in Central America, in 1838* (New York: Wiley & Putnam, 1839); Robert Dunlop, *Travels in Central America* (London: Longman, Brown, Green and Longman, 1847); Frederick Crowe, *The Gospel in Central America* (London: Charles Gilpin, 1850); H. de T. d'Arlach, *Souvenirs de l'Amérique Centrale* (Paris: Charpentier, 1850); Carl von Scherzer, *Travels in the Free States of Central America: Nicaragua, Honduras, and El Salvador* (London: Longman, Brown, Green, 1857); Carl von Scherzer and Moritz Wagner, *La República de Costa Rica en América Central* (Leipzig: Arnoldische, 1856; San José, Costa Rica: Ministerio de Juventud, Cultura y Deportes, 1974); G. F. Von Tempsky, *Mitla: A Narrative of Incidents and Personal Adventures on a Journey in Mexico, Guatemala, and Salvador in the Years 1853 to 1855* (London: Longman, Brown, Green, Longmans & Roberts, 1858); Wilhelm Marr, *Reise Mach Central-Amerika*, 2 vols. (Hamburg: O. Meissner, 1863); Anthony Trollope, *The West Indies and the Spanish Main* (London: Chapman & Hall, 1859; Gloucester: Alan Sutton, 1985); Félix Belly, *A travers l'Amérique Centrale*, 2 vols. (Paris: Librairie de la Suisse Romande, 1867); Arthur Morelet, *Travels in Central America including Some Accounts of Regions Unexplored Since the Conquest* (Paris:

Suggestions for Further Reading

Gide et J. Baudry, 1857; trans. Mrs. M. F. Squier, New York: Laypoldt, Holt and Williams, 1871); Ephraim George Squier, *Nicaragua: Its People, Scenery, Monuments and the Proposed Interoceanic Canal*, 2 vols. (New York: Appleton, 1851; San José, Costa Rica: EDUCA, 1970); Ephraim George Squier, *Notes on Central America* (New York: Harper & Brothers, 1855); John Baily, *Central America* (London: Trelawney Saunders, 1850); William Wells, *Explorations and Adventures in Honduras* (London: Sampson, Low, 1857); Francisco Solano Astaburuaga y Cienfuegos, *República de Centroamérica, o idea de su historia i de su estado actual* (Santiago, Chile: Imprenta del Ferrocarril, 1857; San José, Costa Rica: Talleres Gutenberg, 1929); Julius Froebel, *Seven Years Travel in Central America, Northern Mexico and the Far West of the United States* (London: Richard Bentley, 1859); Mrs. Henry G. Foote, *Recollections of Central America and the West Coast of Africa* (London: T. C. Newby, 1869); Joseph Laferriere, *De Paris a Guatemala* (Paris: Garnier Freres, 1877); and Pablo Lévy, *Notas geográficas y económicas sobre la República de Nicaragua* (Paris: E. Denne Schmitz, 1873; Managua: Banco de América, 1976). Ricardo Fernández Guardia compiled a useful selection of travelers' accounts of Costa Rica in *Costa Rica en el siglo XIX: Antología de viajeros*, (San José, Costa Rica: EDUCA, 1970). A similar collection for El Salvador is Rafael Menjívar and Rafael Guidos Vejar, eds., *El Salvador de 1840 a 1935* (San Salvador: UCA Editores, 1978).

Autobiographies

An equally indispensable, if highly partisan and "traditional," source is the series of autobiographies or historical/interpretive works written by leading statesmen of the time. Perhaps the most interesting figure, and surely the most prolific, is Lorenzo Montúfar y Rivera Maestre, *Reseña histórica de Centroamérica*, 7 vols. (Guatemala: Tipografía El Progreso, 1878–1888); and his *Memorias autobiográficas* (Guatemala, 1898; San José, Costa Rica: Libro Libre, 1988). Other classic commentators on the early independent period include Alejandro Marure, *Efemérides de los hechos notables acaecidos en la República de Centroamérica desde 1821 hasta 1842*, 2 vols. (Guatemala: Imprenta de la Paz, 1844; Ministerio de Educación Pública, 1956), and *Bosquejo histórico de las revoluciones de Centroamérica*, 2 vols. (Guatemala: Tipografía "El Progreso," 1877); Manuel José Arce, *Memoria del General Manuel José Arce* (San Salvador: Ministerio de Cultura, 1959) and *Breves indicaciones sobre la reorganización de Centroamérica* (San Salvador: Tipografía "La Unión," 1905); and from the seldom heard Conservative position, Manuel Montúfar y Coronado, *Memorias para la historia de la revolución de Centroamérica* (Jalapa, Mexico: Aburto y Blanco, 1832).

An account by a key participant in the 1871 revolution is given by Miguel García Granados, *Memorias del General Miguel García Granados* (Guatemala:

Ministerio de Educación Pública, 1952). The broadest chronological coverage can be found in Antonio Batres Jáuregui, *La América Central ante la historia, 1821–1921,* 3 vols. (Guatemala: Tipografía Sánchez y De Guise, 1920, 1949). A curious combination of biography and "collected works" is available for the Salvadoran leader Francisco Dueñas in Diego Rodríguez, *Artículos políticos del Doctor Francisco Dueñas, Ex-Presidente de la República (precedidos de una biografía)* (San Salvador: Dutriz Hermanos Editores, Tipografía La Unión, 1905). The autobiography of Manuel Gallardo, a nominal Conservative, prosperous coffee planter, and French-educated physician, is found in Miguel Angel Gallardo, ed., *Papeles históricos,* Volume I (Santa Tecla, El Salvador: n.p., 1954). A highly partisan view of Salvadoran Liberal leader Francisco Menéndez is offered by Francisco Castañeda, *El General Menéndez y sus victimarios* (San Salvador: Dirección General de Publicaciones, 1966).

The Economy

Materials with which to study the basic economic patterns and activities of Central America during this time period have grown substantially in the past generation. Ralph Lee Woodward, Jr., provides a survey of the economy in the late colonial period in "The Economy of Central America at the Close of the Colonial Period," in *Estudios del Reino de Guatemala,* ed. Duncan Kinkead (Seville: Escuela de Estudios Hispanoamericanos, 1985), 117–34. For the economy in the late eighteenth century see also Wilbur Eugene Meneray, "The Kingdom of Guatemala during the Reign of Charles III, 1759–1788" (Ph.D. diss., University of North Carolina, 1975); Francisco Solano y Pérez Lila, "Tierra, comercio y sociedad (un análisis de la estructura social agraria durante el siglo XVIII)," *Revista de Indias* 125–26 (December 1971): 311–65; Miles Wortman, "Bourbon Reforms in Central America, 1750–1786," *The Americas* 32 (October 1975): 222–38, and "Government Revenue and Economic Trends in Central America, 1787–1819," *Hispanic American Historical Review* 55 (May 1975): 251–86; Victor Hugo Acuña Ortega, "Capital comercial y comercio exterior en América Central durante el siglo XVIII: una contribución," *Estudios sociales centroamericanos* 26 (1980): 71–102; and Adriaan C. Van Oss, "El régimen autosuficiente de España en Centro América," *Mesoamérica* 3 (June 1982): 67–89; "La población de América Central hacia 1800," *Anales de la academia de geografía e historia de Guatemala* 55 (1981): 291–311; and *Catholic Colonialism: A Parish History of Guatemala, 1524–1821* (London: Cambridge University Press, 1986).

For a case study of the intendency system see Thomas Marc Fiehrer, "The Baron de Carondelet as Agent of Bourbon Reform: A Study of Spanish Colonial Administration in the Years of the French Revolution" (Ph.D. diss., Tulane University, 1977). Early mining is discussed by Troy Floyd in "Bourbon Palliatives and the

Suggestions for Further Reading

Central American Mining Industry, 1765–1800," *The Americas* 18 (1961): 103–25. The economy of Costa Rica is discussed in Thomas L. Karnes, "The Origins of Costa Rican Federalism," *The Americas* 15 (1959): 249–69. An illuminating printed source for the economy and society in the late colonial period in Guatemala and El Salvador is the report written by the Bishop Pedro Cortés y Larraz. The portion referring to El Salvador was reprinted as "Descripción geográfico-moral de la Provincia de San Salvador en la Diocesis de Gohatemala," in El Salvador, Ministerio de Relaciones Exteriores, *Colección de documentos importantes relativos a la República de El Salvador* (San Salvador: Imprenta Nacional, 1921). Also for El Salvador, the single best printed source on the state of the economy before Independence is Antonio Gutiérrez y Ulloa, *Estado general de la Provincia de San Salvador* (San Salvador: Dirección de Publicaciones, 1962).

For a view of early independent trade patterns see Robert Naylor, "British Commercial Relations with Central America, 1821–1851" (Ph.D. diss., Tulane University, 1959). Statistical and anecdotal information on the economy immediately after independence can be found in George A. Thompson, *Narrative of An Official Visit*.

The first major synthetic statement on the history of coffee cultivation, written in the mid-1970s, was by Ciro F. S. Cardoso, "La historia económica del café en Centroamérica (siglo XIX): Estudio comparativo," *Estudios sociales centroamericanos* 4 (1975): 9–55. A recent synthesis that focuses largely on post-1870 developments but that also includes new material on earlier times is by Robert Williams, *States and Social Evolution: Coffee and the Formation of National Governments in Central America* (Chapel Hill: University of North Carolina Press, 1994).

Monographic research on coffee includes work on Costa Rica by Carolyn Hall, *El café y el desarrollo histórico-geográfico de Costa Rica* (San José, Costa Rica: Editorial Costa Rica, 1976); *Cóncavas: Formación de una hacienda cafetalera, 1889–1911* (San José, Costa Rica: Editorial Universidad de Costa Rica, 1978); Ciro Cardoso, "The Formation of the Coffee Estate in Nineteenth-Century Costa Rica," in *Land and Labor in Latin America: Essays on the Development of Agrarian Capitalism in the Nineteenth and Twentieth Centuries*, ed. Kenneth Duncan and Ian Rutledge (London: Cambridge University Press, 1977), 165–202; Lowell Gudmundson, *Costa Rica Before Coffee: Society and Economy on the Eve of the Export Boom* (Baton Rouge: Louisiana State University Press, 1986); and Mario Samper Kutschbach, *Generations of Settlers: A Study of Rural Households and Markets on the Costa Rican Frontier, 1850–1935* (Boulder, Colo.: Westview Press, 1990).

On El Salvador the classic study was by David Browning, *El Salvador: Landscape and Society* (London: Clarendon Press, 1971). See also David Alejandro Luna, *Manual de historia económica de El Salvador* (San Salvador: Editorial Universitaria, 1971), and Derek Kerr, "The Role of the Coffee Industry in the History of El Salvador, 1840–1906" (M.A. thesis, University of Calgary, 1977). More recent studies by Héctor Lindo-Fuentes, *Weak Foundations: The Economy of El Salvador in the Nineteenth Century, 1821–1898* (Berkeley: University of California Press, 1990), and Aldo Antonio Lauria Santiago, "An Agrarian Republic: Production, Politics, and the Peasantry in El Salvador, 1740–1920" (Ph.D. diss., University of Chicago, 1992), substantially alter the framework and timing of coffee-driven agrarian change in El Salvador.

Work on coffee and export agriculture in Guatemala has been led by Julio Castellanos Cambranes and David McCreery. Castellanos Cambranes' major work is *Coffee and Peasants: The Origins of the Modern Plantation Economy in Guatemala, 1853–1897* (Stockholm: Institute of Latin American Studies, 1985), and McCreery's many different articles are synthesized and extended in his forthcoming *Rural Guatemala, 1760–1940*. An earlier and insightful work was by Sanford Mosk, "The Coffee Economy of Guatemala, 1850–1918," *Inter-American Economic Affairs* 9 (1955): 6–20. Early industry in Guatemala is discussed in Paul Jaime Dosal, "Dependency, Revolution and Industrial Development in Guatemala, 1821–1986" (Ph.D. diss., Tulane University, 1987).

An earlier generation based its understanding of both indigo and cochineal production and trade on the classic works by Troy Floyd, starting with his "Salvadorean Indigo and the Guatemalan Merchants" (Ph.D. diss., University of California, Berkeley, 1959), and continuing with his articles, "The Guatemalan Merchants, the Government, and the Provincianos," *Hispanic American Historical Review* 41 (1961): 90–110; and "The Indigo Merchant: Promoter of Central American Economic Development, 1750–1808," *Business History Review* 39 (1965): 466–88; as well as those by Robert Smith, "Indigo Production and Trade in Colonial Guatemala," *Hispanic American Historical Review* 39 (1959): 181–211; and "Forced Labor in the Guatemalan Indigo Works," *Hispanic American Historical Review* 36 (1956): 319–28; Ralph Lee Woodward, *Class Privilege and Economic Development: The Consulado de Comercio of Guatemala, 1793–1871* (Chapel Hill: University of North Carolina Press, 1966); and Miles Wortman, *Government and Society*. However, more recent works by Lindo-Fuentes, *Weak Foundations*, McCreery, *Rural Guatemala*, Aldo Lauria, "An Agrarian Republic," and, in particular, José Antonio Fernández, "To Color All the World Blue: The Indigo Boom and the Central American Market" (Ph.D. diss., University of Texas at Austin, 1992), substantially alter much of the received wisdom on dye production and marketing.

Manuel Rubio Sánchez, *Historia del añil o xiquilite en Centro América*, 2 vols. (San Salvador: Dirección de Publicaciones, 1976), reprints numerous sources on indigo. For an actor's account of the cochineal industry see Robert Dunlop, *Travels in Central America*. Manuel Aguilar, "Memoria sobre el cultivo del café arreglada a la práctica que se observa en Costa Rica," *Revista de Historia* (Costa Rica) 14 (1986): 203–14, is a reprint of an 1845 pamphlet on coffee cultivation techniques, and an even earlier "practical guide" to coffee planting can be found in A. B. C. Dumont, *Consideraciones sobre el cultivo del café en esta isla* (Havana, Cuba: Imprenta Fraternal, 1823), reprinted by the Gálvez regime in Guatemala in 1833 by the Imprenta de la Unión.

Honduran mining in the 1850s is described in detail by William Wells,

Suggestions for Further Reading

Explorations and Adventures. For a later period see Kenneth Vergne Finney, "Precious Metal Mining and the Modernization of Honduras: In Quest of El Dorado (1880–1900)" (Ph.D. diss., Tulane University, 1973). For the impact of the U.S. Civil War on the economy of Guatemala, see Ralph Lee Woodward, Jr., "Guatemalan Cotton and the American Civil War," *Inter-American Economic Affairs* 18 (1964): 87–94. For the development of the railroad network, see Delmer G. Ross, "The Construction of the Railroads of Central America" (Ph.D. diss., University of California, Santa Barbara, 1970). For information on the history of money and banking, see John P. Young, *Central American Currency and Finance* (Princeton: Princeton University Press, 1925), and for a numismatic approach see Charles M. Robinson III, *The Coins of Central America, 1733–1965* (San Benito, Tex.: Charles M. Robinson III, 1965); and Alcedo F. Almanzar and Brian R. Stickney, *The Coins and Paper Money of El Salvador* (San Antonio, Tex.: Almanzar's Coins of the World, 1973).

Studies of the institutional context for economic growth, or lack of it, are few in number. Particularly important in this area are the works by Woodward, *Class Privilege*; Williams, *States and Social Evolution*; Lindo-Fuentes, *Weak Foundations*; David McCreery, *Development and the State in Reforma Guatemala, 1871–1885* (Athens, Ohio: Ohio University Center for International Studies, 1983); and Iván Molina's various studies of land sales, titling, credit, and politics in Costa Rica, most easily accessible in *La alborada del capitalismo agrario en Costa Rica* (San José, Costa Rica: Editorial Universidad de Costa Rica, 1988); and *Costa Rica (1800–1850): El legado colonial y la génesis del capitalismo* (San José, Costa Rica: Editorial de la Universidad de Costa Rica, 1991). Equally important, perhaps, are the studies of "unofficial," family-based trade networks and their transformation; see Gustavo Palma Murga, "Núcleos de poder local y relaciones familiares en la ciudad de Guatemala a finales del siglo XVIII," *Mesoamérica* 12 (1986): 241–308; and Miles Wortman, Diana Balmori, and Stuart F. Voss, *Notable Family Networks in Latin America* (Chicago: University of Chicago Press, 1984).

Relatively few studies deal with overall national economies or with activities neither tied to exports (cattle raising in particular) nor easily taxable (mining and lumbering). This makes for a particularly weak basis with which to view Nicaraguan and Honduran economic history. Several of the titles discussed below in reference to the Atlantic coastal regions and peoples shed light on these issues but by definition in regions virtually outside the nation-state framework at the time. In addition, we do know that these economic activities were of considerable importance within the space of the emerging Ladino state structure. The few studies that break this silence are as follows: for Nicaragua see David Radell, "Historical Geography of Western Nicaragua" (Ph.D. diss., University of California, Berkeley, 1969); and Alberto Lanuza, "La formación del Estado nacional en Nicaragua: Las bases económicas, comerciales y financieras entre 1821 y 1873," in *Economía y sociedad en la construcción del Estado en Nicaragua*, ed. Alberto Lanuza, Juan Luis Vázquez, Amaru Barahona, and Emilia Chamorro (San José, Costa Rica: Instituto

Suggestions for Further Reading

Centroamericano de Administración Pública [ICAP], 1983), 7–138; and "La minería en Nicaragua (1821–1875)," *Anuario de estudios centroamericanos* 3 (1977): 215–24; and José Luis Velázquez, "La incidencia de la formación de la economía agroexportadora en el intento de formación del Estado nacional de Nicaragua, 1860–1930," *Revista Conservadora* 32 (1977): 11–31; for Costa Rica see Lowell Gudmundson, *Hacendados, precaristas y políticos: La ganadería y el latifundismo guanacasteco, 1800–1950* (San José, Costa Rica: Editorial Costa Rica, 1983); and for Honduras see Héctor Pérez Brignoli, "Economía y sociedad en Honduras durante el siglo XIX," *Estudios sociales centroamericanos* 6 (1973): 51–82; C. A. Brand, "The Background of Capitalist Underdevelopment, Honduras to 1913" (Ph.D. diss., University of Pittsburgh, 1972); and José Guevara Escudero, "Nineteenth-Century Honduras: A Regional Approach to the Economic History of Central America, 1839–1914" (Ph.D. diss., New York University, 1983).

Independence and Federation

Nearly all classic studies of Liberal/Conservative conflict were written by Liberal partisans such as Montúfar. The scholarly literature more recently relied on Ralph Lee Woodward's, "Economic and Social Origins of the Guatemalan Political Parties (1773–1823)," *Hispanic American Historical Review* 45 (1965): 544–66 and his reevaluation of Carrera in "Social Revolution in Guatemala: The Carrera Revolt," in *Applied Enlightenment: Nineteenth-Century Liberalism, 1830–1839*, ed. Margaret A. L. Harrison and Robert Wauchope, Middle American Research Institute, no. 23 (New Orleans: Tulane University, 1971), 43–70.

Works that analyze the conflicts of independence and the federation include Wortman, *Government and Society*; Louis E. Bumgartner, *José del Valle of Central America* (Durham, N.C.: Duke University Press, 1963); Franklin D. Parker, *José Cecilio del Valle and the Establishment of the Central American Confederation* (Tegucigalpa: Universidad de Honduras, 1955); Carlos Meléndez Chaverri, *José Cecilio del Valle, sabio centroamericano* (San José, Costa Rica: Libro Libre, 1984); Mario Rodríguez, *The Cádiz Experiment in Central America, 1808 to 1826* (Berkeley: University of California Press, 1978); Gordon Kenyon, "Mexican Influence in Central America, 1821–1823," *Hispanic American Historical Review* 41 (1961): 175–205; Robert S. Smith, "Financing the Central American Federation, 1821–1838," *Hispanic American Historical Review* 43 (1963): 483–510; Philip Flemion, "States' Rights and Partisan Politics: Manuel José Arce and the Struggles for Central American Union," *Hispanic American Historical Review* 53 (1973): 600–618; and "Manuel José Arce and the Formation of the Federal Republic of Central America" (Ph.D. diss., University of Florida, 1969); Miriam Williford, "Las luces y La Civilización: The Social Reforms of Mariano Gálvez," in *Applied Enlightenment*, 33–41; and "The Educational Reforms of Dr. Mariano Gálvez," *Journal of Inter-*

Suggestions for Further Reading

American Studies 10 (1968): 461–73; Antonio Batres Jáuregui, *El Doctor Mariano Gálvez y su época*, 2nd ed. (Guatemala: Ministerio de Educación Pública, 1957); Edgar Escobar Medrano, *Mariano Rivera Paz y su época* (Guatemala: Universidad de San Carlos, 1982); Jorge Luis Arriola, *Gálvez en la encrucijada* (Mexico City: Editorial Costa Amic, 1961); and Julio Pinto Soria, *Centroamérica, de la colonia al Estado nacional (1800–1840)* (Guatemala: Editorial Universitaria, 1986).

Standard works on the federation period (1824–1838) and Francisco Morazán begin with Thomas Karnes, *The Failure of Union: Central America, 1824–1960* (Chapel Hill: University of North Carolina Press, 1961); and Alberto Herrarte, *La unión de Centroamérica*, 2nd ed. (Guatemala: Ministerio de Educación Pública, 1963). Other useful works include Rodrigo Facio, *Trayectoria y crisis de la federación centroamericana* (San José, Costa Rica: Imprenta Nacional, 1949); P. J. Chamorro y Zelaya, *Historia de la federación de la América Central, 1823–1840* (Madrid: Ediciones de Cultura Hispánica, 1951); Constantino Láscaris, *Historia de las ideas en Centroamérica* (San José, Costa Rica: EDUCA, 1970); Andrés Townsend Ezcurra, *Las Provincias Unidas de Centroamérica: Fundación de la República*, 2nd ed. (San José, Costa Rica: Editorial Costa Rica, 1973); Lorenzo Montúfar, *Morazán* (San José, Costa Rica: Editorial Costa Rica, 1970); R. S. Chamberlain, *Francisco Morazán, Champion of Central American Federation* (Coral Gables: University of Miami Press, 1950); and Ramón Rosa, *Historia del Benemérito Gral. Don Francisco Morazán* (Tegucigalpa: Instituto Morazánico, 1971).

The early historiography surrounding these conflicts is discussed by Franklin D. Parker in "The Histories and Historians of Central America to 1850" (Ph.D. diss., University of Illinois, 1951). Key printed sources for the independence period are found in Carlos Meléndez Chaverri, ed., *Textos fundamentales de la Independencia Centroamericana* (San José, Costa Rica: EDUCA, 1971). Also useful are República de Costa Rica, *Documentos históricos posteriores a la Independencia* (San José, Costa Rica: Imprenta María v. de Lines, 1923); *Archivo Histórico de El Salvador* (San Salvador: Imprenta "Rafael Reyes," 1923); and Vicente Filisola, *La cooperación de México en la Independencia de Centro América* (Mexico City: Librería de la vda. de Ch. Bouret, 1911). The constitutions issued in that period are reprinted in Ricardo Gallardo, *Las constituciones de la República Federal de Centro-América*, 2 vols. (Madrid: Instituto Estudios Políticos, 1958).

For two decades the standard work on the rise of Carrera and his neo-Conservative coalition was the doctoral thesis by Hazel M. B. Ingersoll, "The War of the Mountain: A Study of a Reactionary Peasant Insurgency in Guatemala, 1837–1873" (Ph.D. diss., George Washington University, 1972). Carrera was subsequently portrayed as a popular hero by E. Bradford Burns, *The Poverty of Progress: Latin America in the Nineteenth Century* (Berkeley: University of California Press, 1980), and by Keith L. Miceli, "Rafael Carrera: Defender and Promotor of Peasant Interests in Guatemala, 1837–1848," *The Americas* 31 (1974): 72–95. No equivalent exaltation of Carrera emerged in Guatemala itself, although his figure was effectively rehabilitated by Manuel Coronado Aguilar, "El General Rafael

Carrera ante la Historia," *Anales de la academia de geografía e historia* (Guatemala) 28 (1965): 217–61, in the face of several generations of Liberal historiographic defamation. Pedro Tobar Cruz, *Los montañeses* (Guatemala: Ministerio de Educación Pública, 1959), and *Los montañeses: Facción de los Lucíos* (Guatemala: Editorial Universitaria, 1971), was also highly critical of the pro-Liberal simplifi-cations of mid-nineteenth-century history but stopped short of embracing a pro-Carrera position. Moreover, he substantially raised the level of research by his example. The biography of Carrera by Ralph Lee Woodward, Jr., *Rafael Carrera and the Emergence*, returns Carrera to a redeemed but not exalted state. In *Caudillos in Spanish America, 1800–1850* (Oxford: Clarendon Press, 1992), John Lynch de-votes a chapter to Carrera, and although he has little information that would surprise Central Americanists, it is a useful exercise to see Carrera in the context of his contemporaries in the caudillo business.

Other studies of the Conservative era in Guatemala include Arturo Taracena Arriola, "Estado de los Altos, indígenas y régimen conservador: Guatemala, 1838–1851," *Avances de Investigación*, no. 64 (Universidad de Costa Rica: Centro de Investigaciones Históricas, 1993); Luis Beltranena Sinibaldi, *Fundación de la República de Guatemala* (Guatemala: Tipografía Nacional, 1971); Ralph Lee Woodward, Jr., "The State and the Indian in Conservative Guatemala, 1838–1871," paper presented at the Annual Meeting of the Latin American Studies Association, New Orleans, March 17–19, 1988; and "Liberalism, Conservatism, and the Response of the Peasants of La Montaña to the Government of Guatemala, 1821–1850," *Plantation Society in the Americas* 1 (1979): 109–29; Michael Fry, "Política agraria y reacción campesina: La región de la montaña, 1821–1838," *Mesoamérica* 15 (1988): 25–46; Juan Carlos Solórzano, "Rafael Carrera, Reacción conservadora o revolución campesina? Guatemala, 1837-1873," *Anuario de estudios centroamericanos* 13 (1987): 5–35; José Arzú, *Pepe Batres íntimo: su familia, su correspondencia, sus papeles* (Guatemala: Tipografía Sánchez y De Guise, 1940); Antonio Batres Jáuregui, *José Batres Montúfar; su tiempo y sus obras* (Guatemala: Tipografía Sánchez y De Guise, 1910); and David Chandler, *Juan José de Aycinena: Idealista conservador de la Guatemala del siglo XIX* (Antigua: CIRMA, 1988).

The Liberal Revolutions

Surprisingly, the 1871 Revolution has been poorly studied as a purely political phenomenon, with most attention paid to its subsequent economic or social policies. A good example of this tendency is the article by Augusto Cazali Avila, "El desarrollo del cultivo del café y su influencia en el régimen del trabajo agrícola: Etapa de la reforma liberal, 1871–1885," *Anuario de estudios centroamericanos* 2 (1976). However, several works provide either insights in essay form or materials on monographic topics relevant to Liberalism's eventual triumph. Two of the more modest but insightful essays are by Marco A. Villamar Contreras, *Apuntes sobre la Reforma Liberal* (Guatemala: Departamento de Publicaciones, Universidad de San Carlos, 1977); and Jorge Arriola, "Evolución y revolución en el movimiento liberal de 1871," *Anales de la academia de geografía e historia* (Guatemala) 49 (1976): 99–121.

The traditional Liberal view is effectively represented by the classic study by Jorge M. García Laguardia, *La Reforma Liberal en Guatemala* (San José, Costa Rica: EDUCA, 1972); and the hagiographic tradition can be seen in José Santos Noriega, *Barrios, el pacificador* (Guatemala: Delgado, Impresos y Cía, 1983). A more substantial biography of Barrios is by Paul Burgess, *Justo Rufino Barrios: A Biography* (Philadelphia: Dorrance & Co., 1926). The economic policies of Barrios are analyzed in Thomas R. Herrick, *Desarrollo económico y político de Guatemala durante el periódo de Justo Rufino Barrios (1871–1885)* (Guatemala: Editorial Universitaria, 1974). Although no effective study of the background to the revolution is available, Wayne Clegern's essay, "Transition from Conservatism to Liberalism in Guatemala, 1865–1871," in *Hispanic American Essays in Honor of Max Leon Moorehead*, ed. W. Coker (Pensacola, Fla.: Perdido Bay Press, 1979), provides important details; they are greatly expanded in his new book, *Origins of Liberal Dictatorship in Central America: Guatemala: 1865–1873* (Boulder: University Press of Colorado, 1994). The memoirs of Miguel García Granados are also an important source.

Studies of Liberal/Conservative conflicts elsewhere in Central America are somewhat less abundant. For El Salvador major sources include Lindo-Fuentes, *Weak Foundations*; Aldo Lauria, "An Agrarian Republic"; E. Bradford Burns, "The Modernization of Underdevelopment: El Salvador, 1858–1931," *Journal of Developing Areas* 18 (1984): 293–316; Ricardo Gallardo, *Las constituciones de El Salvador*, 2 vols. (Madrid: Ediciones Cultura Hispánica, 1961); and of more importance, Italo López Vallecillos, *Gerardo Barrios y su tiempo*, 2 vols. (San Salvador: Ministerio de Educación, 1967). The best source for printed documents on this period in El Salvador is the idiosyncratically organized multivolume work by Miguel Angel García, *Diccionario histórico-enciclopédico de la República de El Salvador* (San Salvador: Imprenta Nacional, various dates). Other printed sources for El Salvador are found in Lorenzo López, *Estadística general de la República de El Salvador, 1858* (San Salvador: Dirección de Publicaciones, 1974); José D. Gámez, *Gerardo Barrios ante la posteridad* (Managua: Tipografía Nacional, 1901); and María Leistenschneider, ed., *Dr. Rafael Zaldívar. Recopilación de documentos históricos relativos a su administración* (San Salvador: Dirección de Publicaciones, 1977).

For Nicaragua there are studies by E. Bradford Burns, *Patriarch and Folk: The Emergence of Nicaragua, 1798–1858* (Cambridge: Harvard University Press, 1991); Emilio Alvarez Lejarza, "El Liberalismo en los 30 Años," *Revista conservadora del pensamiento centroamericano* 51 (1964): 23–35; Juan Luis Vázquez, "Luchas políticas y Estado Oligárquico," in *Economía y sociedad en la construcción del Estado*

Suggestions for Further Reading

en Nicaragua, ed. Juan Luis Vázquez, Alberto Lanuza, Amaru Barahona y Emilia Chamorro (San José, Costa Rica: Instituto Centroamericano de Administración Pública [ICAP], 1983), 139–206; and Orlando Cuadra Downing, *Bernabé Somoza (1815–1849): Vida y muerte de un hombre de acción* (Managua: Imprenta Nacional, 1970). See also the relevant sections in Jaime Wheelock Román, *Imperialismo y dictadura* (Mexico City: Siglo Veintiuno Editores, 1975).

For Costa Rica an influential interpretation is found in Carlos Monge Alfaro, *Historia de Costa Rica* (San José, Costa Rica: Imprenta Trejos Hnos., 1966). A challenge to this traditional interpretation of Costa Rican history is found in Lowell Gudmundson's monograph, *Costa Rica Before Coffee*, and other important works include Carlos Meléndez Chaverri, *Dr. José María Montealegre* (San José, Costa Rica: Editorial Costa Rica, 1968); and Rodolfo Cerdas Cruz, *Formación del Estado en Costa Rica* (San José, Costa Rica: Editorial de la Universidad de Costa Rica, 1964; 2nd ed., San José, Costa Rica: Editorial Costa Rica, 1978).

Few studies have explored the complexities of Liberal and Conservative land tenure policies and their considerable similarities. Chief among them are McCreery, *Rural Guatemala*; Castellanos Cambranes, *Coffee and Peasants*; Lindo-Fuentes, *Weak Foundations*; Aldo Lauria, "An Agrarian Republic"; Gudmundson, *Costa Rica Before Coffee*; and Samper Kutchbach, *Generations of Settlers*. Rafael Menjívar, *Acumulación originaria y el desarrollo del capitalismo en El Salvador* (San José,Costa Rica: EDUCA, 1980), attempts to quantify the extent of land transfer in El Salvador as a result of the 1879–1881 Liberal policies, following Browning's study, but the estimation is based on data from such disparate periods that the results are flawed. Two Costa Rican studies of, respectively, public lands acquisition and the attack on Indian common lands are also relevant in comparison with other regions. See José Antonio Salas Víquez, "La privatización de los baldíos nacionales en Costa Rica durante el siglo XIX: Legislación y procedimientos utilizados para su adjudicación," *Revista de Historia* (Costa Rica) 15 (1987): 63–118; and Margarita Bolaños Arquín, "La lucha de los pueblos indígenas del Valle Central por su tierra comunal, siglo XIX" (Master's thesis, Universidad de Costa Rica, 1986). For an extraordinarily revealing, if confused, account by a first-hand observer of the land tenure policies pursued by Carrera and the Liberals who followed see the work of one of the leading agrimensores of the time, Luis Wolfram, *Principios elementales de la economía social sobre la civilización de los pueblos y los progresos de la agricultura* (Guatemala: Tipografía La Estrella, 1887).

Challenges to Liberalism

The question of Liberal failures in the creation of a national identity prior to the 1880s has been brilliantly analyzed by Steven Palmer, "A Liberal Discipline: Inventing Nations in Guatemala and Costa Rica, 1870–1900" (Ph.D. diss., Colum-

144

bia University, 1990), chapter 3. Studies on the nemesis of Liberal secularism, the Church, begin with classic works by Mary Wilhelmine Williams, "The Ecclesiastical Policy of Francisco Morazán and the Other Central American Liberals," *Hispanic American Historical Review* 3 (1920): 119–43; and Mary P. Holleran, *Church and State in Guatemala* (New York: Columbia University Press, 1949). The high point of 1830s conflict between the Church and the state was analyzed by Mario Rodriguez, "The Livingston Codes in the Guatemalan Crisis of 1837–1838," in *Applied Enlightenment*, 1–32. On the cholera epidemics of the nineteenth century see Germán Tjarks et al., "La epidemia del cólera de 1856 en el Valle Central: análisis y consecuencias demográficas," *Revista de Historia* (Costa Rica) 3 (1976): 81–129; and Victor Cruz Reyes, "Epidemias del siglo XIX en Honduras," *Mesoamérica* 6 (1985): 371–90.

Church-state conflict in the era of Liberal triumph has been studied by Hubert J. Miller, *La Iglesia y el Estado en tiempo de Justo Rufino Barrios* (Guatemala: Editorial Universitaria, 1976); and Gustavo Palma Murga, "Algunas relaciones entre la Iglesia y los grupos particulares durante el período de 1860 a 1870: Su incidencia en el movimiento liberal de 1871" (Licenciatura thesis, Universidad de San Carlos, 1977). Mauricio Domínguez T., "El Obispado de San Salvador: Foco de desavenencia político-religiosa," *Anuario de estudios centroamericanos* 1 (1974): 87–134, recounts the Salvadoran bishopric campaigns and controversies. Information on the Jesuits is provided by P. Santiago Malaina, S.J., *La Compañía de Jesús en El Salvador, C.A.* (San Salvador: Imprenta Nacional, 1939), and Rodolfo Cardenal, *El poder eclesiástico en El Salvador, 1871–1931* (San Salvador: UCA Editores, 1980), continues the story thereafter. The question of the expropriation of Church property throughout the period has been studied only in Costa Rica so far, by Yamileth González García, "Desintegración de bienes de cofradías y de fondos píos en Costa Rica, 1805–1845," *Mesoamérica* 5 (1984): 279–303; and Lowell Gudmundson, "La expropiación de las obras pías en Costa Rica, 1805–1860," in Gudmundson, *Hacendados*, 17–71. For Nicaragua see Franco Cerutti, *Los Jesuitas en Nicaragua en el siglo XIX* (San José, Costa Rica: Libro Libre, 1984).

Foreign Influences

On foreign colonization schemes, xenophobic local responses, and the foreign role more generally, the most important source for the early independent period remains the work by William Griffiths, *Empires in the Wilderness: Foreign Colonization and Development in Guatemala, 1834–1844* (Chapel Hill: University of North Carolina Press, 1965); and "The Livingston Codes in the Guatemalan Crisis of 1837–1838," in *Applied Enlightenment*, 1–32. A printed source on foreign colonization schemes is Compagnie Belge de Colonization, *Amerique Centrale Colonisation du District de Santo-Thomas de Guatemala* (Paris: Rignoux, 1844).

145

Suggestions for Further Reading

Mario Rodríguez, *A Palmerstonian Diplomat in Central America, Frederick Chatfield, Esq.* (Tucson: University of Arizona Press, 1964), provides a full biography of the single most controversial figure of the time and leaves no doubts as to why radical Liberals loved to hate this particular symbol of British power. For another view see Robert Naylor, "The British Role in Central America Prior to the Clayton-Bulwer Treaty of 1850," *Hispanic American Historical Review* 40 (1960): 361–82. Thomas Karnes, *The Failure of Union*, provides the basic chronology of Central American disunion in this period, and Charles Stansifer, "The Central American Career of E. G. Squier" (Ph.D. diss., Tulane University, 1959), discusses the role of the North American envoy who first sought to counter Chatfield's policies but eventually came to rival him as a focus of antiinterventionist feeling in Nicaragua. A Spanish version of this work is "Ephraim George Squier: diversos aspectos de su carrera en Centroamérica," *Revista conservadora del pensamiento centroamericano* 20 (November 1968).

David Folkman, *The Nicaragua Route* (Salt Lake City: University of Utah Press, 1972), is the standard account of the background to the Walker fiasco, and R. E. May, *The Southern Dream of a Caribbean Empire, 1854–1861* (Baton Rouge: Louisiana State University Press, 1973), places the episode in its larger context. The chief protagonist's own views are still in print as William Walker, *The War in Nicaragua* (Tucson: University of Arizona Press, 1985). An account of Carrera's patterns of influence over Guatemala's neighbors is offered by Ralph Lee Woodward, Jr., "La política centroamericana de Rafael Carrera, 1840–1865," *Anuario de estudios centroamericanos* 9 (1983): 55–68.

For the economic aspects of foreign penetration of the region, see the detailed studies of Thomas and Ebba Schoonover, "Statistics for an Understanding of Foreign Intrusions into Central America from the 1820s to 1930," *Anuario de estudios centroamericanos* 15 (1989): 93–118; 16 (1990): 135–56; 17 (1991): 77–119. Information on particular diplomats and economic policies can also be found in Thomas Schoonover, *The United States in Central America, 1860–1911: Episodes of Social Imperialism and Imperial Rivalry in the World System* (Durham, N.C.: Duke University Press, 1991).

The Ethnic Dimension

Ethnic identity and differentiation in the core areas of Central America have been of increasing interest to scholars. An enlightening contemporary theoretical statement can be found in Philippe Bourgois, *Ethnicity at Work: Divided Labor on a Central American Banana Plantation* (Baltimore: Johns Hopkins University Press, 1989). The essential colonial background has been sketched admirably by Christopher Lutz, *Historia sociodemográfica de Santiago de Guatemala, 1541–1773*, Serie Monográfica no. 2 (Antigua: CIRMA, 1982), recently published in English in amplified form as *Santiago de Guatemala, 1541–1773: City, Caste, and the Colonial Experience* (Norman: University of Oklahoma Press, 1994). An overview of the entire period appears in Robert Carmack, "Spanish-Indian Relations in Highland Guatemala, 1800–1944," in *Spaniards and Indians in Southeastern Mesoamerica: Essays on the History of Ethnic Relations*, ed. Murdo MacLeod and Robert Wasserstrom (Lincoln: University of Nebraska Press, 1983), 215–52. An innovative argument for the nineteenth-century origins of the Ladino/Indian dichotomy in Guatemala has been put forward by Carol Smith, "Origins of the National Question in Guatemala: An Hypothesis," in *Guatemalan Indians and the State, 1540 to 1988*, ed. Carol A. Smith (Austin: University of Texas Press, 1990), 72–95. For the position of the African-American population in Ladino society and its evolution, see Lutz, *Historia sociodemográfica*, and Lowell Gudmundson, "Black into White in Nineteenth-Century Spanish America: Afro-American Assimilation in Argentina and Costa Rica," *Slavery and Abolition* 5 (1984): 35–49.

For the evolution of the multiethnic peripheries of Central America in this period, in particular the Atlantic coast, perhaps the best introductory essay is by Charles R. Hale, "Relaciones interétnicas y la estructura de clases en la costa atlántica de Nicaragua," *Estudios sociales centroamericanos* 48 (1988): 71–91. The most basic interpretive works are by Mary Helms, "Of Kings and Contexts: Ethnohistorical Interpretations of Miskito Political Structure and Function," *American Ethnologist* 13 (1986): 506–603; and *Asang: Adaptations to Culture Contact in a Miskito Community* (Gainesville: University Presses of Florida, 1971); Nancy L. González, *Sojourners of the Caribbean: Ethnogenesis and Ethnohistory of the Garifuna* (Urbana: University of Illinois Press, 1988); and Jorge Jenkins Molieri, *El desafío indígena de Nicaragua: el caso de los miskitos* (Mexico City: Editorial Katún, 1986). Michael Olien, "Miskito Kings and the Line of Succession," *Journal of Anthropological Research* 39 (1983): 198–241, focuses more narrowly on the royal succession question and the allegations of British imperial manipulation of same, and Rebecca Bateman, "Africans and Indians: A Comparative Study of the Black Carib and Black Seminole," *Ethnohistory* 37 (1990): 1–24, offers a highly suggestive comparison of the experiences of mixed African-Indian populations in Central America and the United States. For a major pioneering study of the peripheral indigenous societies of the Petén in northern Guatemala see Norman Schwartz, *Forest Society: A Social History of Petén* (Philadelphia: University of Pennsylvania Press, 1990).

Other authors have focused on the economic, political, and diplomatic histories of the Atlantic coastal regions. The best of the group is the study by Craig L. Dozier, *Nicaragua's Mosquito Shore: The Years of British and American Presence* (Tuscaloosa: University of Alabama Press, 1985). Less successful but informative studies include Robert Naylor, *Penny Ante Imperialism: The Mosquito Shore and the Bay of Honduras, 1600–1914: A Case Study in British Informal Empire* (Cranbury, N.J.: Fairleigh Dickinson University Press, 1988), and Jorge Jenkins Molieri, "La Mosquitia nicaragüense: Articulación de una formación precapitalista: Su historia (Partes I y II)," *Estudios sociales centroamericanos* 26 (1980). On Belize and coastal Honduras, in addition to the works by González and Bateman, see Nigel Bolland,

147

Suggestions for Further Reading

The Formation of a Colonial Society: Belize, from Conquest to Crown Colony (Baltimore: Johns Hopkins University Press, 1977); and Wayne Clegern, *British Honduras: Colonial Dead End, 1859–1900* (Baton Rouge: Louisiana State University Press, 1967).

Historical Geography

Studies that illuminate the historical geography and the social history of the family and household in Central America's diverse regions are relatively recent, although at least one classic source and inspiration is Rodolfo Barón Castro, *La población de El Salvador* (Madrid: Consejo Superior de Investigaciones Científicas, 1942). More recent pioneering works include Carolyn Hall, *Costa Rica: A Geographical Interpretation in Historical Perspective* (Boulder, Colo.: Westview Press, 1985); Robert Carmack, *The Quiché Mayas of Utatlán: The Evolution of a Highland Guatemalan Kingdom* (Norman: University of Oklahoma Press, 1981); John D. Early, *The Demographic Structure and Evolution of a Peasant System: The Guatemalan Population* (Boca Raton: University Presses of Florida, 1982); Robert Carmack, John Early, and Christopher Lutz, eds., *The Historical Demography of Highland Guatemala*, Institute for Mesoamerican Studies, no. 6 (Albany: State University of New York, 1982), 371–90; and Jean Piel, *Sajcabaja: Muerte y resurrección de un pueblo de Guatemala, 1500–1970* (Mexico City: CEMCA, 1989).

An analysis of the unique human ecology and occupational diversity of highland indigenous settlement can be found in several of Carmack's works, as well as in Carol Smith, "Local History in Global Context: Social and Economic Transitions in Western Guatemala," *Comparative Studies in Society and History* 26 (1984): 193–228. However, the most succinct statement of the parcialidad system of dispersed settlement is by Nancy Farriss, "Nucleation versus Dispersal: The Dynamics of Population Movements in Colonial Yucatán," *Hispanic American Historical Review* 58 (1978): 187–216. Overviews of Guatemalan population and family history in the nineteenth century can be found in Ralph Lee Woodward, Jr., "Population and Development in Guatemala, 1840–1870," *SECOLAS Annals, Journal of the Southeastern Council on Latin American Studies* 14 (1983): 5–18, and Norbert Ortmayr, "Matrimonio, Estado y sociedad en Guatemala (siglo XIX y XX)," in *Territorio y sociedad en Guatemala: tres ensayos históricos* (Guatemala: Ediciones CEUR, Universidad de San Carlos, 1991). Work on the history of Guatemala City is effectively summarized by Gisela Gellert and Julio Pinto Soria, *Ciudad de Guatemala: Dos estudios sobre su evolución urbana (1524–1950)* (Guatemala: Universidad de San Carlos, Editorial Universitaria, 1992). A more general treatment of urbanization and the economics of settlement patterns in Guatemala can be found in Carol Smith, "The Domestic Marketing System in Western Guatemala: An Economic, Locational, and Cultural Analysis" (Ph.D. diss., Stanford University,

1972), and "El desarrollo de la primacía urbana, la dependencia en la exportación y la formación de clases en Guatemala," *Mesoamérica* 5 (1984): 195–278.

For analyses of Costa Rican settlement patterns and household composition in the 1840s, see Gudmundson, *Costa Rica Before Coffee*. For colonization zones and interfamilial economic ties the best source is Mario Samper, *Generations of Settlers*. For more recent research on family size and age at marriage see Eugenia Rodríguez Sáenz, "Padres e hijos: Familia y mercado matrimonial en el Valle Central de Costa Rica (1821–1850)," in *Héroes al gusto y libros de moda: Sociedad y cambio cultural en Costa Rica (1750–1900)*, ed. Iván Molina and Steven Palmer (San José, Costa Rica: Editorial Porvenir, 1992), 45–76; and for inheritance patterns Lowell Gudmundson, "Peasant, Farmer, Proletarian: Class Formation and Inheritance in a Smallholder Coffee Economy, 1850–1950," *Hispanic American Historical Review* 69 (1989): 221–57.

Index

Acajutla, El Salvador, 27, 36, 37, 39, 41
Accessory Transit Company, 38
African Americans, 118, 121, 123–25
Agrimensores (land surveyors), 9-10, 117
Aguilar, Eugenio, 108
Alcabala, 69, 70. *See also* Taxes
Alcaldes mayores, 19, 20, 21
Amapala, Honduras, 69
Amatitlán, Guatemala, 44–45, 98
Antigua, Guatemala, 44–45
Aquino, Anastasio, 83
Arce, Manuel José, 70, 91, 108
Artisanry: and impact of imports 113–14
Aycinena, Juan José, 91, 108
Aycinena, Marquis of, 15

Baldíos, 24, 50. *See also* Land tenure
Bananas, 41, 43
Banks, 33, 35, 46, 75, 103
Barclay, Herring and Richardson, 70
Barrios, Gerardo, 92, 97, 99, 103, 108
Barrios, Justo Rufino, 50, 51, 87, 91, 95, 97, 118–19
Barrundia, José Francisco, 87, 131 (n. 31)
Barrundia, Juan, 87
Belize, 29–30, 36–37, 39, 63, 67, 69
Bourbon reforms: and the Church, 101–2
Bourgois, Philippe, 6, 125
Browning, David, 98
Bulmer-Thomas, Victor, 13
Burns, E. Bradford, 5, 6, 9, 128–29 (n. 4)
Bushnell, David, 6

Calandracas, 92
California, 36–38, 73, 98–99
Callao, Peru, 37
Canacos, 121
Capellanías, 21, 101–3. *See also* Credit
Carrera, Rafael, 4, 9–10, 12 (n. 10) 80–83, 86, 89–92, 95–97, 103–5, 109
Carrillo, Braulio, 87, 97
Cartago, Costa Rica, 83, 117
Casáus y Torres, Ramón, 91, 103, 105

Castellanos Cambranes, Julio, 3, 97
Cattle, 13, 20, 24, 33, 39, 43, 53– 55, 66– 67, 70, 75, 111–12, 123–25
Censo, 101– 3
Censo enfitéutico, 97. *See also* Land tenure
Cerna, Vicente, 92, 97
Chalatenango, El Salvador, 65
Chatfield, Frederick, 67, 80, 86, 89
Chinandega pact, 86
Chiquimula, Guatemala, 95, 98
Cholera epidemics, 109
Choluteca, Honduras, 53
Chontales, Honduras, 53
Church. *See* Roman Catholic Church
Clarence, Robert Henry, 126
Cochineal, 31, 33, 43–45, 63, 95
Coffee, 10, 45–53; and banks, 35; and credit, 34, 45; and economic growth, 10, 33; and ethnicity, 121–22; exports, 43, 63, 74; impact of, 1, 10, 24; and internal trade, 64, 67; and investment, 25, 31, 33, 42; and labor, 25, 42; and land tenure, 25, 42, 93–100; and the tithe, 103; oligarchies and, 53, 75; prices of, 42; state organization and, 58, 72, 75; taxes and, 70–72; transportation of, 39, 41
Cofradías, 21, 101–103
Comayagua, Honduras, 38, 39, 82
Communal lands, 9, 11, 14, 24–25, 50, 92–95. *See also* Baldíos; Ejidos; Land tenure
Conservatives, 1, 3, 4, 5, 9, 10, 43, 73, 75, 79–83, 86–93, 97, 99–100, 103–4, 106, 109, 127–28
Consolidación de Vales Reales (1804), 101
Corregidores, 23
Cortés y Larraz, Pedro, 80
Costa Cuca, 93
Costa Rica: banks, 35; Church question in, 103, 107, 109–10; coffee in, 25, 52, 74; credit in, 34–35, 46; currency, 35; entrepreneurship in, 52; ethnicity in,

151

Costa Rica (*continued*)
120–21, 125; exports, 42, 61, 63, 69, 72; historiography of, 1, 3–4, 6, 8; impact of war on, 30–31; imports, 63; inheritance in, 119; internal trade in, 65, 68, 69; investment in, 31; labor in, 24, 28, 50–51, 74; land tenure in, 25, 95–97, 99; land registry, 46; Liberal-Conservative conflict in, 82, 86–87, 90, 92–93, 127; population and settlement types, 22–24, 46, 111–18; ports, 27, 36–37; taxes, 70–71; trade, 20, 67; transportation, 39–41, 51

Cotton, 26, 43, 63, 67

Credit: cattle and, 53–54; censo enfitéutico, 45; cochineal and, 44–45; coffee and, 34, 46–53, 58; during colonial period, 20–22; habilitación system, 20–21, 33–34, 56, 64; and indigo trade, 19–22, 44; internal trade and, 64–65, 73; investment climate and, 34; land tenure and, 25; merchant, 15–16, 19, 27, 29, 33; Montepío de Cosecheros de Añil, 19, 21, 22, 28; regional trade and, 31; Roman Catholic Church as provider of, 21, 101–3; rubber and, 56; scarcity of, 14; sugar and, 54

Cruz, Serapio, 83

Cruz, Vicente, 83

Cuba, 4, 39, 52, 53

Currency, 35, 61

Dávila, Fernando Antonio, 91, 114, 116

Debt peonage, 18, 23. *See also* Labor

Dependency theory, 4, 6–7

Desamparados, Costa Rica, 99

Desnudos, 83, 92

Divorce, 104–5, 119–20

Dog Law (Ley de perro), 105

Dominicans, 101–104

Dueñas, Francisco, 91, 93, 97–98, 103

Dunlop, Robert, 44, 45, 95, 112

Education: Conservative policies and Liberal critique, 106–107; Liberal initiatives, 107; Pavón Law, 107

Ejidos, 14, 24–25, 50. *See also* Land tenure

El Salvador: banks 36; Church question in, 101, 108; coffee in, 42, 48, 50; cotton in, 63; credit in, 34; currency, 35; ethnicity in, 120, 123, 125; exports, 61–62; fairs and internal trade in, 65–69;

historiography of, 1, 3–4, 6, 8; impact of war on, 30–31; indigo trade in, 16, 19–20; labor in, 24, 48; land tenure in, 25, 50, 96–98, 100; land registry, 46; Liberal-Conservative conflict in, 83, 86–87, 91–93; population and settlement types, 22, 24, 111–13, 116; ports, 27, 38; taxes, 71; transportation, 39, 41

Encomienda, 23. *See also* Labor

Escobar, Narciso, 117

Escuintla, Guatemala, 98

Esquipulas, Guatemala, 65, 67

Ethnicity: and geographic distribution, 111–12, 120–21 and "whitening," 123–25; identity and terminologies, 120–25

Evans, Peter, 7

Exchange rates, 61

Exports: impact on society of, 13, 72–76, 114, 116, 127–28; private land ownership and, 92–95; reorientation toward, 27; statistics, 59–63; taxes and, 69, 72; transportation and, 15–16, 34, 36–37. *See also* Trade, internal

Fairs, 64–69; cattle sold in, 53; credit and, 19–20, 34; and indigo trade, 19–20. *See also* Trade, internal

Federal Republic of Central America, 1–2; cochineal production, 44; currency, 35; economic policies, 29–30; expropriation of Church wealth, 102–103; immigration, 50; ports, 36; tax policies, 69–70; wars, 29

Federation. *See* Federal Republic of Central America

Fernández Guardia, Ricardo, 111

Fiebres, 87

Flores, Cerilo, 87

Flores Flores, José, 119–20

Gallardo, Manuel, 93

Gálvez, Mariano, 12 (n.10), 31, 45, 91, 95, 102, 104, 108–9, 126

Garcia Granados, Miguel, 50, 87

Gold. *See* Mining

Gold rush, 10, 37, 38, 93, 98

Golfo Dulce, 15, 27, 35

Granada, Nicaragua, 27, 60, 83, 114

Guardiola, Santos, 86

Guatemala: banks, 35; Church question in, 101–5, 107–8; cochineal in, 31, 44–45; coffee in, 42; cotton in, 63; credit in, 20–21, 33–34, 48; ethnicity in, 121–23;

exports, 61–62; historiography of, 1, 3–4, 6–9; impact of wars on, 30–31; indigo trade in, 16, 20; internal trade and fairs in, 65, 67; labor in, 22, 24, 28, 50–51; land tenure in, 24–25, 50, 93–98, 100; land registry, 46; Liberal-Conservative conflict in, 82–83, 86–87, 90–91; merchant elite, 14–16, 20; population and settlement types, 22–23, 112–14, 116; ports, 27, 36–37; taxes, 70–71; transportation, 35, 39, 41

Guatemala City, 82, 96, 98, 106, 112, 120–21

Guerra de las Comunidades (Nicaragua), 83

Gulf of Honduras, 15, 27, 39

Gulf of Nicoya, Costa Rica, 67

Habilitación system. *See* Credit

Hacienda, 8, 14, 24, 25, 28, 54. *See also* Land tenure

Hacienda Serijiers (Guatemala), 122

Hale, John, 63

Hall, Carolyn, 52

Halperín Donghi, Tulio, 12 (n. 1), 31, 79

Heredia, Costa Rica, 115

Herrera, Dionisio, 121

Honduras: banks, 35; cattle in, 53–54; colonial trade and, 19–20; ethnicity in, 121; exports, 43, 61–62; historiography of, 4, 8; internal trade and fairs in, 65–69; impact of war on, 30–31; land tenure in, 93–96; Liberal-Conservative conflict in, 82, 86, 91; mining in, 54–56; population and settlement types, 22, 24, 112–13; ports, 27, 39; transportation, 41; taxes, 71; wood in, 57–58, 95

Household composition, 117–18

Immigration, 50

Imports, 20, 29–30, 63–64, 67, 92, 113–14

Indian population: artisanry and, 113–14, 116; compulsory labor and, 15, 28, 51, 59; credit and, 34; distribution of, 96, 111–12, 116, 120, 124–25; ethnic reclassification of, 120–21, 124; land belonging to, 25, 50, 97–98; market participation of, 26; statistics, 23–24

Indigo: credit and financing of, 19, 33–34; exports of, 43; fairs and, 65–66; impact of war on, 30; investment in, 18; labor demands, 19, 22; processing, 17–18, 33;

production and trade, 16–20, 44; transportation costs, 41

Inheritance: rights and legislation, 104, 118–19; patterns in Costa Rica, 119

Interest rates, 33–34

Investment: cattle and, 43; coffee and, 25, 46–48; impact of war on, 30, 33–35; indigo and, 18; land and, 25; land tenure and, 51; mining and, 55; sugar and, 54

Iturbide, Agustín de, 29

Iturrios (priest of Chinautla, Guatemala), 88

Izabal, Guatemala, 27, 36, 39, 67

Iztapa, Guatemala, 36, 37, 39

Jamaica, 125–26

Jury trial, 104–5

Juticalpa, Honduras, 56

Labor, 11, 18, 22–24, 28, 30. *See also* Debt peonage; Encomienda; Repartimiento

Ladino: origin and meaning of term, 121–22

Lake Nicaragua, 16, 27, 38

La Libertad, El Salvador, 36

Land registries, 46, 47, 51, 58

Land tenure, 8, 11, 14, 24–25, 50; policies of Conservatives, 8–11, 12 (nn. 8, 10); and conflict with Liberals, 93–100. *See also* Baldíos; Communal lands; Ejidos

La Unión, El Salvador, 36, 38, 39, 66

León, Nicaragua, 83, 86, 89, 90, 114

Lévy, Pablo, 56, 57, 60

Liberal reforms, 1–6, 9–11, 13, 25, 63, 75, 92–93, 103, 118–20, 125–28

Liberals, 2–10, 43, 51, 75, 79–83, 86–97, 99–104, 106–10, 118–19, 126–28

Lindo-Fuentes, Héctor, 93, 97–98, 112

Livingston Codes, 89, 104, 105

Llorente y Lafuente, Anselmo, 103, 109–10

Logging. *See* Wood

Los Altos, 87–89, 91, 112, 114, 120, 129 (n. 9)

Lucíos, 83, 104

Lutz, Christopher, 123

Macaulay, Neil, 6

Malespín, Francisco, 86, 91–92

Mallon, Florencia, 7

Marr, Wilhelm, 68, 121

Marriage: access to and age at, 116, 124;

Index

and race mixture, 121, 123; Liberal legislation on, 105–6
Marure, Alejandro, 30
Matagalpa, Nicaragua, 53
Matina, Costa Rica, 27
Mayorazgo, 119
McCreery, David, 3
Mechudos, 83, 92
Medina, Crisanto, 103
Menjívar, Rafael, 98
Merchants: cotton production and, 63; credit and, 20–22, 33, 66; foreign, 28, 45, 52, 63, 69; role of, 15–16, 19; rubber trade and, 56; and trade routes, 27, 35, 37
Mexico, 7, 87–88, 90
Mining, 54–56; export agriculture and, 30; exports, 43
Miskitos, 58. *See also* Zambo
Molina, Iván, 74
Money. *See* Currency
Montealegre, José María, 51, 93, 95
Montepío de Cosecheros de Añil. *See* Credit
Montúfar, Lorenzo, 88–89, 105
Montúfar, Manuel, 29
Mora, Juan Rafael, 51, 87, 90, 93, 95, 103, 109, 110, 121
Morazán, Francisco, 80, 81, 83, 91, 95, 103, 104, 121
Mosquito chief (Robert Henry Clarence), 126
Mosquito Coast, 89, 124–25
Muñoz, José Trinidad, 91
Muybridge, Edweard, 122

Nicaragua: banks, 35; cattle in, 53–54; Church question in, 103; coffee in, 61; cotton in, 63; credit in, 33; currency, 35; ethnicity in, 120–21, 125; exports, 43, 60–63; historiography of, 4, 8, 90, 92; impact of war on, 31; indigo production and trade in, 16, 19–20; internal trade and fairs in, 65; land tenure in, 93–95; Liberal-Conservative conflict in, 82–83, 87, 90–92; mining in, 66; population and settlement types, 22, 23, 112, 113; ports, 27, 36, 39; rubber in, 56; sugar in, 54; taxes, 71; trade in, 20; transoceanic route, 38; transportation, 41; William Walker invasion of, 38–39, 89, 91, 92; wood in, 57–58

Obras pías, 21
Occupational distribution: and impact of exports/imports, 113–14
Olancho, Honduras, 39, 65
Omoa, Honduras, 27, 36, 39, 65, 66, 69

Pacific Mail Steamship Company, 38, 41, 69
Palencia, Guatemala, 104
Palmar, Quetzaltenango, 117
Palmer, Steven, 6, 109
Panama, 15, 20, 27, 37, 38
Panama Railroad, 13, 38, 41, 73
Parcialidad, 116
Pavón, Manuel F., 107
Pérez Brignoli, Héctor, 12 (n. 4), 13, 127
Pérez, Jerónimo, 92
Peru, 7, 37, 66
Petén, 120, 124
Pineda Mont, Rafael, 119
Population: distribution and growth rates, 116, 124; pyramid (Costa Rica), 115; size (Central America), 113
Ports, 27, 36–42, 51, 72. *See also* individual ports
Prostitution, 120
Puerto Cortés, Honduras, 41
Pulpero, 121
Puntarenas, Costa Rica, 27, 36, 37, 39, 40, 51

Quetzaltenango, 67, 87, 91, 117

Railroads, 36, 39–41, 72
Rancherías, 117
Realejo, Nicaragua, 27, 36, 37
Remincheros, 83
Repartimiento, 18, 23, 28. *See also* Labor
Repartimiento de bienes, 19, 26
Rincón, 116–17
Rivas, Patricio, 91
Rivera Paz, Mariano, 94
Roads, 31, 36, 39, 51, 56, 69, 72
Rodríguez, Mario, 5
Roman Catholic Church, 11; cofradías, 21; credit and, 21, 28; land and, 24; Liberal attacks on, 95, 100–10; San Salvador Bishopric and, 100–1, 108
Rosa, Ramón, 106
Rubber, 43, 53, 56–57, 75

Sacatepéquez, 88
Safford, Frank, 82, 87

Index

Samper Kutschbach, Mario, 3, 12 (n. 4), 46
San Gerónimo sugar estate, 102
San Isidro, Guatemala, 122
San José, Costa Rica, 39, 68, 83, 99, 111, 117
San José, Guatemala, 37, 39, 41
San Juan del Norte, Nicaragua, 27, 39
San Juan River, 15, 27, 38, 43, 56
San Luis, Guatemala, 37
San Miguel, El Salvador, 22, 38, 39, 65, 66, 67
San Pedro Sula, Honduras, 41
San Salvador, 82, 86–89, 108, 114
San Vicente, El Salvador, 38, 65, 69
Santa Anna, El Salvador, 22, 90
Santa María, Quetzaltenango, 117
Santo Tomás, Guatemala, 27
Sarsaparilla, 26, 43
Segovia, Nicaragua, 53
Serviles, 92
Shepherd brothers, 125
Silver. See Mining
Skocpol, Theda, 7
Smith, Carol, 6, 96, 121, 128 (n. 3)
Sociedad Económica Itineraria, 51
Somoza, Bernabé, 83
Sonsonate, El Salvador, 22, 39, 69
Squier, Ephraim George, 37, 65
Stein, Barbara, 14
Stein, Stanley, 14
Sugar, 26, 54, 67

Talamanca, Costa Rica, 124
Taracena, Arturo, 129 (n. 9)
Taxes, 8, 29–30, 60, 66, 69–72
Tegucigalpa, Honduras, 38, 39, 69, 82
Textiles, 26, 29, 64, 68, 112, 114, 116
Thompson, George A., 33

Timbucos, 92
Tobacco, 20, 43, 67, 70, 71, 112
Tobar Cruz, Pedro, 83
Totonicapán, Guatemala, 83
Trade, internal, 25–29, 112–14. See also Fairs
Transportation. See Railroads; Panama Railroad; Roads; Ports; Pacific Mail Steamship Company
Tribute, 23, 26
Trujillo, Honduras, 27, 36, 39, 65

United Fruit Company, 4
Urtecho, José Coronel, 89–90

Valle, José Cecilio del, 26, 29
Valparaíso, Chile, 27, 37
Vanderbilt, Cornelius, 38, 39
Van Oss, Adriaan, 24
Vasconcelos, Doroteo, 91
Veracruz, 21, 27
Verapaz, 120
Viteri y Ungo, Jorge, 108

Walker, William, 80, 86–87, 89–92, 104, 109
War: economic impact of, 30–31, 70; social bases of, 82–83, 87–93
Wolfram, Luis, 9, 12 (n. 10)
Wood, 39, 43, 57–58, 62; and logging concessions, 95, 125
Woodward, Ralph Lee, Jr., 3
Wortman, Miles, 95

Yucatán, 88

Zambo (zambo-mosquito), 121, 123–24
Zelaya, Francisco, 65
Zelaya, José Santos, 51, 93

About the Authors

Lowell Gudmundson is Professor and Chair of Latin American Studies, Mount Holyoke College. He received a bachelor's degree from Macalester College, a master's from Stanford University, and a doctorate from the University of Minnesota. He is author of *Estratificación socio-racial y económica de Costa Rica, 1700–1850* (1978), *Hacendados, precaristas y políticos: La ganadería y el latifundismo guanacasteco, 1800–1950* (1983), *Costa Rica Before Coffee: Society and Economy on the Eve of the Export Boom* (1986), co-author of *El judío en Costa Rica* (1979), and co-editor of *Coffee, Society and Power in Latin America* (1995).

Héctor Lindo-Fuentes is Associate Professor of History, Fordham University. He received a bachelor's degree from Universidad Centroamericana José Simeon Cañas, San Salvador, and his master's and doctorate from the University of Chicago. He is author of *Weak Foundations: The Economy of El Salvador in the Nineteenth Century* (1990), and co-editor of *Historia de El Salvador* (1994).

156